COLLEGE OF MARIN LIBRARY
KENTFIELD, CALIFORNIA

P9-ECR-485

THE OTHER
Martin Buber

THE OTHER
Martin Buber

RECOLLECTIONS OF HIS
CONTEMPORARIES

Haim Gordon

OHIO
UNIVERSITY
PRESS

Introduction © Copyright 1988 by Haim Gordon.
Printed in the United States of America.
All rights reserved.
Ohio University Press books are printed on acid-free paper. ∞

Library of Congress Cataloging-in-Publication Data
Gordon, Hayim.
    The other Martin Buber : recollections of his contemporaries /
Haim Gordon.
        p.   cm.
    ISBN 0-8214-0907-7
    1. Buber, Martin, 1878–1965. 2. Philosophers, Jewish—
Germany—Biography. 3. Philosophers—Germany—
Biography. 4. Jews—Germany—Biography. I. Title.
B3213.B84G65   1988
181'.06—dc19
{B}   86-5979
                                                                CIP

Designed by Laury A. Egan

For Rivca

Contents

CONTENTS

Introduction

Behind the interviews collected in this volume is a story of a search for realization, a process that in all probability would have pleased Martin Buber. After writing a Ph.D. dissertation on Buber's philosophy of education, I became intrigued by the question of whether Buber's educational philosophy could be realized. At that time, I believed, quite naively, that Martin Buber surely had realized his own educational thought, and therefore I started interviewing his students and contemporaries about him as an educator. I was wrong. Like many of us, and perhaps even more than many of us, Buber had problems implementing his own educational philosophy. What is more, he seemed to be a rather poor teacher. In short, the reality I found was much more complex than I had imagined it to be.

In studying Buber the educator, I discovered that Buber the person had not been at all exposed to the public eye. He belonged to a generation in Germany that was very private, a phenomenon that has been documented in quite a few scholarly studies. In this respect Buber was a child of his generation. Thus in those activities of everyday life where dialogue was called for, where one may encounter the "Thou," the advocate of dialogue and of the "I-Thou" relationship was unknown to his readers. This discovery encouraged me to continue my interviews with Buber's contemporaries and his family, so that the people Buber had known could testify as to the aspects of his life that do not appear in his writings. I must admit that at the same time I also continued to search for hints as to how Buber's philosophy could be realized.

This story has two endings. I myself struggled to realize Buber's educational thought by teaching Jews and Arabs to relate to each other through dialogue in the spirit of Martin Buber's philosophy. But I could not embark on this project until I understood that I would have to find my own way of realizing Buber's philosophy. My many failures and few successes are documented in another book (*Dance, Dialogue, and Despair: Existentialist Philosophy and Education for Peace in Israel,* University of Alabama Press, 1986). The other ending is this book. Here an entire new dimension of Martin Buber emerges, a Buber much different from the image we derive from just reading *I and Thou* or *Tales of the Hasidim* or *Between Man and Man* or any of his other books, including his autobiographical fragments, not only because Buber was more complex than those writings convey, but also because the complex interactions described by the interviewees have to do with the everyday encounters that make up a person's life.

Thus, this book is both a re-visioning of Buber's image and a tribute to him. It definitely reveals that Martin Buber was not the great master of dialogue that some of his admirers and idolizers strove to present. On the other hand, he was an engaged, concerned person, who in his own manner strove to cope with the difficult reality confronting him. Often he made mistakes and deserves to be criticized, and indeed many of the respondents voiced their criticism of him. However, his mistakes were those of a person who was making history through his writings, research, and actions. In other words, Buber should be remembered as a living person, not only as an oracle hidden behind his writings, and it is the memories and recollections of his contemporaries that help us remember Buber the man.

The interviewees often had a problem remembering events that occurred decades ago, and I have no doubt that some of them have added their own interpretations of the events they recalled. Thus this book presents raw data; in the process of editing the interviews I have attempted to keep that rawness intact. Despite the rawness, some of Buber's characteristics stand out, reappearing again and again. Many people found that Buber could concentrate on relating to them, but that he still seemed to be insensitive to them as people. A few of them suggest that perhaps Buber knew that it was important to relate to other people, but because of his immersion in intellectual activities he had to tear himself away from his work in order to relate dialogically. Others felt that this insensitivity had deeper sources. However, all interviewees agree that a person only rarely felt relaxed in Buber's company. Meeting him was an engagement, a task, a commitment, a responsibility, and Buber's personality seemed to demand that it be so.

In the twenty-seven interviews with Buber's (nonfamily) contemporaries, one finds only two women. This probably is partially a result of the patriarchal milieu in which Buber lived, but it also seems to support the thesis that Buber himself had problems interacting with women, as Jochanan Bloch and Moshe Shpitzer testified. Buber's daughter and granddaughters indicate that Buber seemed to regard womanhood as a kingdom of its own, in which he did not feel comfortable.

Both characteristics suggest a general point that emerges only slowly, as one reads and rereads the interviews, and that was perhaps best expressed by Ben Ami. Buber's popularity, his eloquent and dramatic public speaking, his successes and good fortune throughout his life—all these cannot conceal the fact that Martin Buber was a lonely person. Ben Ami remembers an almost impenetrable circle of loneliness surrounding Buber. Note that not one of the respondents describes Buber as a friend, or describes the relations between Buber and himself or herself as a friendship. Jochanan Bloch even recalls that when Buber died he felt almost a relief, because only then did he feel capable of writing his book on Buber. Although one might suggest that the formality of relations in Germany could be the basis of this loneliness, such an answer would be superficial. As Bloch, Kraft, Yeari, and others who grew up in the same milieu suggest, Buber was lonely because he did not know how to share his weaknesses and difficulties with others. His loneliness had much to do with himself, and not only with the milieu in which he was nurtured.

Many respondents agree that Buber was an important influence on their lives, either through his writings or through his actions. Whether Buber's presentation of himself was a pose, as Jochanan Bloch suggests, or an authentic mode of being, as Michael Wyschogrod testifies, both clearly admit that they were deeply influenced by their encounters with Buber. Hence, even if Buber did not realize his own dialogical philosophy, as not a few interviewees suggest, his personality did influence the lives of many. It was not only his charm, but also his often imposing presence that demanded that other people respond to him as a person and as a thinker. But this occurred primarily when one met personally with Buber. It did not occur when he taught, as all of his students testified; but it could occur when he gave a public lecture. Buber seemed unaware of the instances in which he did influence people and of the moments in which his influence was minimal. Perhaps it did not concern him.

Today, about ten years after conducting the interviews, I probably would ask different questions. One of them, especially to members of the family, but also to students and colleagues, would have been: Did you love Buber? I do not know what the answer would have been, but on the basis of the material in this book, I believe it would have been revealing. From these interviews one learns that Buber was not a person who expected to be loved; but he did expect to be listened to very carefully; and he was. Was he loved? Did he love? And whom?

Much more research is needed before we can clearly discern Martin Buber, the man. This book, these interviews, are one more perspective to be taken into account when a definitive biography of Buber is written.

The interviews were held in the years 1976–1979. Many of the persons interviewed have since died. All interviewees were told that their recollections of Buber probably would be shortened or edited before being published (as I did in preparing this book) and that I might use some of the material merely as background data for other publications (as I have done). Several people refused to be interviewed, among them Raphael Buber, Martin Buber's son, and Margot Cohen, Buber's secretary for the last six years of his life; his colleagues Nathan Rotenstreich and Gershom Scholem also refused. The interviews were held in Hebrew, and I have made every effort in the translation to present the intention of the interviewees.

PART I

Family

First Interview with Judith Agassi-Buber

(Martin Buber's Granddaughter)

Q. I understand that you and your sister grew up in Buber's house. Can you explain how that happened?

A. When my parents were divorced, Buber acquired a court injunction making him and Grandmother the formal guardians of my sister and myself. So from the age of four I have memories of growing up in Buber's house in Heppenheim.

Q. Did Buber take part in your education?

A. Not really. He was our formal guardian, but day-to-day education was Grandmother's role. He was rather remote, and spent many hours each day in his study. Like many families, we met during meals and when we went on vacation together. Meetings with Grandfather occurred when a crisis arose; they were not daily experiences. The entire area of our physical care and daily upbringing was undertaken by Grandmother. That included contacts with the school, with our friends, etc. When we grew older, our relationship with Grandmother also became more remote.

Q. So you didn't have much personal contact with Buber, even though you grew up in his house?

A. Correct. On holidays or joint vacations we all spent time together, but during the year we were summoned to his study only when we had misbehaved— for instance, not come home on time. In 1933 other children started to curse us and to throw rocks at us in the street; Grandfather summoned us to his study and explained to us what antisemitism is all about, and what is important in Judaism, and why our classmates and other people were acting this way. When my sister and I started believing in Marxism in the

1940s—we were teenagers, already in Israel—Buber called both of us to his study, and explained why our approaches were wrong, especially our belief in the good emanating from what is being done in the USSR. He read us impressions of many persons who had visited the Soviet Union that supported his views. Later I became a student at the Hebrew University and took some courses from Grandfather, and we would discuss the papers I had submitted. As we grew up we began to see that his relations with us were much more spontaneous than with his son (my father) and his daughter. We would say that with each generation Buber's relations with children became more spontaneous. I don't know whether that was true, but one thing is clear. The kind of spontaneity that Buber wrote about and that was central to his thinking, was very difficult for him to express in his relations with my sister and myself.

Q. What do you remember from the period in Heppenheim?

A. I remember that many people would come to visit Grandfather, often people with problems, and that many of them were young. Even though he was strict about his working hours, he would stop everything in order to meet with such a person. This attitude prevailed throughout his entire life, but I remember it especially from my childhood. Frequently, some young people who were hiking through Germany would stop at Heppenheim and come to visit Grandfather. At times, they would even sleep at our home. It seemed to me that everyone wanted to speak with my grandfather. There were also many people who came from far off, and wore all sorts of weird clothing. The story in Heppenheim was that when the railroad station-master saw a person with a turban or a jellaba or any other weird clothing get off the train at Heppenheim, he never waited for the person to ask how to get to Professor Buber's home. He would immediately tell him to go to the right and then turn left at the first corner, and go straight until he reached Buber's house. Buber seemed to thrive on such visits. When he was already well into his seventies or eighties, I remember that when a group of people would come to visit him he would perk up—and even though he had difficulties seeing and hearing, he would participate happily in these meetings, so that people did not realize his old age. There was a glitter in his eyes that appeared only then.

Q. When you grew older, were you impressed by Buber?

A. At times very impressed. For instance, in 1947 I accompanied Grandfather and Grandmother to Europe on a lecture tour that Grandfather gave. We visited Denmark, Sweden, England, France, and Switzerland. That was the first time I saw Buber as a guest lecturer. He was charming and eloquent, and there was a grace to his speeches, but he was also an actor. His lectures were extremely well prepared, including the dramatic moments. What impressed me was how he could do it in so many different languages, and could thus keep large audiences in many countries enthralled with his presentation. He knew Hebrew and German very well—but that did not surprise me. In German he was very strict with his choice of phrases, and there were many discussions with Grandmother on which phrase to choose on a certain occasion. But I was surprised at how well he knew French. I was told that he had known French since childhood. He learned it so thoroughly that his grandfather, Shlomo

Buber, would often enlist Martin's help in his interpretation of Rashi. Rashi often had used French terms when he wrote his commentary to the Bible, and Shlomo Buber, who had no formal education, but was self-taught, would call on his grandson Martin to help him understand these difficult French phrases. And the grandson was a great help.

Q. What about English?

A. Grandfather's English surprised me. He read English freely, but until the Second World War, when *I and Thou* was translated into English by a priest from Scotland, he had had very little contact with spoken English. When the priest started frequenting our house, Buber began speaking English, and learned it. So, in 1947, when he lectured in London to large audiences, English was still not a language with which he was intimately acquainted. Still, he knew how to incorporate into his lecture all those stylistic word plays and polished phrases that characterized his lectures in other languages. Once, during the Second World War, he was approached and asked to lecture for a celebration honoring a jubilee of Copernicus, and to my surprise I heard him lecturing in Polish. Before that I had only heard him speaking Polish with his sister, who by a stroke of luck reached Israel during the war with a section of the Polish army that had been in the Soviet Union.

Q. What other languages did Buber know?

A. He of course knew Latin and Greek, and also Yiddish and Italian. His knowledge of Latin was probably superb. I remember once when I was a student, I asked him if he had a Latin dictionary, and he said no. Then I understood that he knew Latin so well that he had no need of a dictionary. Yiddish, I remember because

6

when we were children, on Sabbath evenings we would read Sholom Aleichem's stories after the Sabbath meal. He was surprised at how few languages our generation knew.

Q. Did you have a regular Sabbath meal?

A. Yes, and Grandmother lit candles every Friday evening. After the meal Grandfather would always read us something. He knew how to read beautifully. When we grew older and Buber learned that we both did not believe in God, I think that it was difficult for him. I recall that Buber did make a Kaddish blessing on Friday evening before the meal for a short period, but it seemed to have troubled him and he stopped.

Q. Were you impressed by the intellectual atmosphere in your grandparents' home? After all, Paula Buber was also an author.

A. Very impressed. The center of the intellectual atmosphere was Grandfather. There were 18,000 books in the house. His study was full of books, but the space there did not suffice. In the second story of the house were a few small rooms that all became part of Buber's library. He worked on translating the Bible in the bedroom. There were two large tables there with all the books and materials he needed, and an adjoining room full of books that had to do with the translation. I remember the ritual. After breakfast he would work until a specific hour on his Bible translation and then come down from the bedroom to his study to work on other topics. During our childhood we did not know what a library was—we had one at home.

Q. What about children's books?

A. We received children's books regularly from some publishers that Grandfather was linked with. But when I said a library I meant novels. In addition to moments of crisis, we would approach Grandfather when we didn't know what to read. He would ask: "Well, have you finished all of Dickens?" and lead us to that shelf. He would only permit us to read certain books. I remember him telling me that Dostoyevski was not for me. That night I took *The Idiot* or *The Brothers Karamazov*—I don't remember which—and read it secretly the entire night, and hid it under my pillow before returning it secretly to the shelf when I woke up.

Q. Did he discuss your readings with you?

A. Yes, and that was an area in which he encouraged me. He would give me compliments concerning my evaluation of what I had read, and then I would feel that I was not a total ignoramus. He was concerned about our education. When all Jewish pupils were kicked out of schools in Germany in 1936, Buber hired a special teacher for us, who was also his part-time secretary, and who started to prepare us for the transfer to Israel. Or much later, in Israel, at the end of the eleventh grade I received a low grade in Arabic. I decided not to make up the grade during the summer vacation, and went to work on a kibbutz, Kibbutz Dalia. But after I had cleared the fields of rocks for a month, a letter arrived from Grandfather, even though there were no paved roads to the kibbutz, and I came home to study.

Q. Were there any quarrels with Buber?

A. Hardly ever. As teenagers we would argue a lot about politics among ourselves and, at times, approach him for his view. I would then usually send my sister to do the talking. We would try to get him involved when we argued with Grandmother about our freedom to go to various places, but he would usually remain aloof.

Q. Did you learn anything from his educational approach?

A. I would not say that he was an example of an educator. My approach to my children is different, very different. He never knew how to play. But I did accept some of his views about teaching. I believe that dialogue is central to teaching, and that adult education is important. Adults can learn and become better persons. I think that both his writings and his deeds in these areas influenced me.

Q. Can you say anything about his friendship with other persons?

A. I know that he had friends who were close to him. But when I knew him, I don't believe he had many close friendships, since he resided in a rather remote area. He did write many letters. People would come to visit Buber, and at times, on vacation, we would meet with some of his friends. I believe that when he was younger his friendships were more intense. From what I heard, at times he would spend weeks with his friends.

Q. Since many people visited Buber in Heppenheim, I understand that often some stayed over and were your guests.

A. Of course. Grandmother had a Swiss approach to receiving guests, and in the house there were many extra beds and mattresses—there were eleven or more rooms in that house. Grandmother always liked us to have enough for all the guests, and that everything should be super clean, and aesthetically pleasing, like the Swiss.

Q. In your approach to life, where do you differ from Buber?

A. I learned from Buber the importance of acquiring—of acquisition as a value—something with which I'm not especially pleased. I would have discussions and at times bitter arguments with him about this. These occurred when I was a student, but I was also interested in politics, and involved myself in political developments in Israel. Buber argues: "You may be right in your wanting to contribute to political developments in Israel, but you can contribute much more if you first become a somebody. For instance, get a M.A. in some field, then you will be somebody in your own right and you will be able to contribute much more to political causes." Being somebody for Buber was not necessarily confined to the academic realm. My sister was a painter. She did not finish high school, but went to study at Betsalel Art School. He supported her: "She will be a somebody in the realm of arts," he said. But I find it a bit sad, if everyone first has to strive to be a somebody, and one cannot relate positively to a person who did not do the maximum to fulfill his potential—even though I do think that we should strive to fulfill our potential.

Q. In educating your children, how did you differ from the education you received in Buber's home?

A. I was more liberal. I was less willing to demand that my children conform to specific rigid rules of behavior. But that approach came from Grandmother. She was rigid, but I mean rigid. She knew what is good and what is bad, what is right and what is wrong—always. In theory Buber knew that imposing such rigidity was wrong, but in practice he went along with it. I believe that he had great difficulties putting himself into the world of young people. I don't want to judge him fully, yet, since I don't yet have grandchildren, but I do try to get into the skin of my own children. As I grow older I can understand the difficulties of the previous generation in understanding us. When my daughter came to me with a totally new approach to life, and presented it to me, it was difficult for me to accept it, and to respond with understanding and with patience. Perhaps Buber faced similar difficulties. And yet I agree with his theoretical view that the educator must develop the good in each young person and not force him to accept the "correct" direction.

Q. Can you say a bit more about tension or quarrels with Buber?

A. There were some when we were teenagers growing up in his house. For instance, when we wanted to go on hikes that he did not approve of, or when we did not work hard enough at our studies. At times, when he was exasperated he would threaten us that he would get in touch with our father. "I can no longer be responsible" he would say.

Q. How was Buber as a family man?

A. His ideal was a family as a small society with many mutual goals. But it remained an ideal and we would joke at his expense, since he was hardly involved with us. His only involvement occurred when we had to move the house with all his books, and we all worked together as a team. But still, he was only involved in packing and moving those thousands of books. He would work with us and smile and say: "Here I see a family working together." But he would not help Grandmother with all the things she had to pack, the household utensils, sheets, etc. I do remember an ad-

ditional instance when he would be involved in family
life with us all: that was in the garden. He had a very
specific role in the upkeep of the large garden around
our house in Heppenheim, although the responsibility for the garden was entirely in Grandmother's
hands. He was in charge of sorting the dahlia bulbs,
cataloging them and labeling them in the fall, and
helping sort them for planting in the spring. That
was PapaMartin's job. He would be called from the
study, and told that the time for work on the dahlias
had come, and he would dedicate himself for hours to
arranging them, writing a note attached to each dahlia,
specifying its type.

Q. You called him PapaMartin?

A. Yes, that was what my sister and I called him. But
returning to joint family ventures, they were mainly
in the mountains, since Buber did not swim. Grandmother was a sportswoman. She swam well and rode
a bike—she was one of the first women, in her student years, to traverse the Alps on a bicycle. Buber
knew how to dance, but he seldom danced. One thing
he did enjoy doing and did for many years was hiking
in the mountains. He was very good at climbing, but
going down was often a problem for him. Each summer we would hike a lot, either in the Swiss Alps or
the Dolomites in Austria and Italy, and also in the
Italian Alps. Here Buber would get very involved. He
would study the maps, decide on where we should
take breaks, and lead us all the way. But when we
took the break, he would not only sit and enjoy the
view and the food we had taken along, he would also
take out the proofs of his Bible translation from one
of his pockets. And from his other pocket would
emerge a Hebrew-German dictionary. Then, in the

midst of the beauty of the Dolomites he would conduct a long discussion with Grandmother on which
word was appropriate for translating a specific verse.

Q. Would you call your childhood in Buber's house a
happy childhood?

A. I'm not sure I would. We did not grow up in an atmosphere where playing was greatly encouraged, and
I often remember, as a child, wanting to meet with
more children. We were a bit impatient with the atmosphere that prevailed.

Q. How did your grandmother feel living with Buber?

A. I really don't know too much about their relations. I
believe that it might have been difficult for Buber to
accept the fact that she was an independent person
who was very active and had succeeded in becoming
an author in Germany. When we moved to Israel she
was cut off from all her previous connections and literary life. She never succeeded in learning Hebrew,
and her German did not help her much in Israel. She
attempted to learn Hebrew, but failed, and that led
to many frustrations. Also, being in charge of the
house in Israel was much more difficult, she had fewer
servants than in Germany, and doing anything in Israel demanded more of her time. She was probably
limited in her contacts, because of the language barrier, to people who came from Germany, and that
brought new frustrations. She was a woman who was
greatly interested in life, especially in stories, and living in Israel with Buber was a frustrating experience
for her, because of the complete change of milieu.

Q. In what respects do you think Buber realized his dialogical philosophy?

A. That is hard to say, and you would need to ask more
specifically. For instance, Buber did try to converse

with simple people, like the tax collector or the grocer. He did not use his family as a means to his ends. But on the other hand, reading Buber may give the impression that Buber could relate easily to children, to other people, or to animals. That is not true. Buber had to make an effort in order to abandon his world of books and turn to other persons. He made a sincere effort, but I am sure that he had difficulties. One must add that he lived a very bourgeois life, and that influenced his entire being. But he was courageous. Once, in Germany during the Nazi reign, the Germans took his passport, and he went by himself to the Gestapo center and asked them why they had taken it. They thought that he was insane in coming to them, but he got his passport back. But he was so work-centered, and so demanding of himself, that it was probably a difficult task for him to open himself to other people.

Q. Which of his writings do you most appreciate?

A. I've read most of them, and I'm not interested in his theological writings, I'm alienated from the religious enterprise that underlies them. I appreciate what he wrote in the realm of society, philology, and history. To an extent I was educated through his translation of the Bible. He taught my sister and myself the Bible, and thus we learned Hebrew from him. I also like his Hasidic stories very much, and believe that "For the Sake of Heaven" is a great book.

Q. Why did you mention Buber being a bourgeois?

A. Because I believe that it throws light on his entire life. He was born to rich parents and grew up in the very affluent household of his grandparents. As a student he was fully supported by his parents and grandparents. He married very young and immediately fathered two children. Perhaps when he began his career there were a few financial problems, but I don't believe that he ever faced the problem of seeking money to pay next month's rent.

Q. So, he lived a very sheltered life?

A. Very. His wife made sure that he had everything on time and in place, from breakfast to the suit he wore. That doesn't mean that he wasn't courageous. He would walk in Jerusalem when it was being shelled, and was not afraid, even though he had never served in the army. Probably he didn't serve because he was too old when the First World War broke out and his health was always delicate, especially his stomach. Yes, he lived a sheltered life, but he was a courageous person.

Q. Did Buber ever discuss with you the reason you and your sister grew up in his house, and not with one of your parents?

A. As far as I remember we never discussed it with him. . . No, not during our childhood years and not with Grandfather. Explanations came only from Grandmother. We knew that our parents had divorced, and later we learned stories of a lawsuit, and that the court had decided that we would grow up in our grandparents' home. My sister lived with my grandparents a bit before the court had decided, since my parents both agreed. My grandparents offered to send her to a famous school in the neighborhood. But after she moved in with them, the doctor suggested that they not send her to school yet, since she had had scarlet fever at the age of four, and at the age of six had not fully recuperated. She continued to live with Grandfather and Grandmother, and they engaged a private teacher for her. She did not go to school until the third grade. I believe that my grandparents didn't mind engaging a private tutor, since their daughter had never gone to school and had been tutored privately. Perhaps Grandmother even preferred this approach. But when my sister reached the third grade she went to school and I went to the first grade—that was after the court decision and I was already living with them. We returned from Italy a bit late for the school year, but we both went to school.

Q. So, Buber never found an opportunity to discuss with you something as important as the reason you lived with him?

A. No. He seemed to shy away from the subject. Only

grandmother discussed our situation with us. The only time Buber and I did discuss this subject seriously was after Grandmother had died, when I was already a mother. Buber had become friendly with my mother, who was living in Germany, and he asked me how my relations with my mother were. I said: "Very good. And she is also playing the role of Grandmother to my daughter very well." He was a bit surprised that this had occurred and mentioned that his own mother had never been a mother to him. His parents had divorced when he was four years old. I told him that there was a significant difference, since my mother never gave up her children willingly, as Buber's mother had done. Quite the opposite. When my mother feared that we would be taken from her, she first ran away with us. Then she fought the lawsuit all along, and did not want to give us up. But when she lost the case, she gave us to Buber. We were in contact with her until I was nine years old. Because of her fleeing the Nazi regime and being in concentration camps, all communication with her was severed. I saw her again when I was twenty-three.

Q. So you think that he compared his own childhood to your childhood?

A. Yes. And perhaps that is the reason he didn't discuss it with us. You see, with him the story was different. His mother's actions led to the divorce, and as a result, I assume that she had few rights. He was separated from her at the age of four and did not have any sort of communication with her until he was thirty-five, when his children were teenagers. Perhaps because he felt closer to his grandparents than to his parents, he thought that this solution would be good for us also. In addition, he was very affluent and had a large house with a garden, while my mother worked in an office and my father started learning to work in a merchant's firm. My father also married again shortly after the divorce. I suspect that Buber believed that in his home we would get better conditions, like the conditions he enjoyed in his grandparents' home.

Q. Did the question every come up later of your moving in with your father?

A. No, not at all. There was no high school at Kibbutz Geva, where my father was a member while we were in high school. In Jerusalem there was a good high school. Grandfather only threatened us with our father when we were fighting over our behavior. I remember a few times that he threatened us when my father already lived in Haifa. He would say: "I can no longer take this, I'll get in touch with your father. . . ." Or: "That's it, the letter to your father is already on my desk. . . ." We did not take these threats seriously. We viewed our father as a sort of older brother.

Q. What do you know about Buber's relations with your father?

A. My father was an adventurous kid. He would disappear from home suddenly. Once he ran away and joined a circus. We heard all these stories from Grandmother, who wrote all kinds of stories, and one of the stories was about a kid called Rafi who did all sorts of things that were nice, but that made his parents worry. My father went to a free progressive school, but said that he learned very little there, and as a result he had great difficulties when he went to high school. There was a lot of tension in the relations between Buber and his son. At the age of fourteen my father had a steady girlfriend, and I'm not sure that they were happy with that. In Heppenheim my father had very

little social life. During the First World War a plane
fell near Heppenheim, and my father went to guard
the plane and caught pneumonia—in short, he got
into trouble frequently. He was bright and promis-
ing, but later his mother was disappointed in his development. Later he became an anti-intellectual, and
wanted to show off that he would work with worldly
things. Buber and Paula did not want him to go into
business, so they sent him to a technical school in Vienna to learn mechanical engineering, especially of
agricultural machines.

Q. Can you say a bit more?

A. He joined the Austrian army at the age of seventeen,
and matriculated after the war at the age of nineteen.
He got involved in politics, and dealt with refugees
from the East. At the age of twenty-one he was already a father. That did not help him to pursue an
academic career. He studied for a year in Mannheim,
practical subjects; during that period he was active in
the Communist youth organization. That generation
was skeptical and cynical toward all the values of their
parents—something like the youth culture of the
1960s in the West. There was a definite generation
gap that was not confined to my father and his father.
My father finally decided to become a practical person, a person who deals with worldly things, the opposite of Grandfather. Dealing with practical things
distanced him from his father. My great-grandfather,
Martin Buber's father, was a man who dealt with
practical things. He managed the large estates that he
owned. He was a good businessman and knew agriculture. Buber was more like his own grandfather,
Solomon Buber, who sat and wrote books while his
wife ran the business. Buber's father did not like the

fact that his son spent so much time on Hasidism and philosophy. In short, my father was more like his grandfather, and Martin Buber, after a while, accepted this. There is a letter from Buber to Raphael where he writes that he is happy that Raphael is successful in the kibbutz. He even added that he hopes that Raphael will soon be able to invite my sister and myself to live with him on the kibbutz. But my sister and I never heard of this letter or this possibility while we were growing up in Buber's house. Perhaps it was not practical.

Q. Did Buber's children get a Jewish education?

A. My father was taught Hebrew. His teacher was S.Y. Agnon, who was then serving as Buber's secretary. They were both also in the Jewish youth movement: Blue-White.

Q. Did you receive any sexual education? Were there any expressions of fondness or love between Buber and Paula?

A. Buber would often fondly call her "Paulaschöne." He would at times kiss her hand. It was clear to us that she was the stronger person in the house, the one who determined things. There were very few expressions of love toward us. When we would meet after a long time or part for an extended period he would kiss our head or pat it and say "A Jewish head." We received absolutely no sexual education, least of all from Buber. All the physical aspects of our life were in the hands of Grandmother. She also had difficulties with the entire topic of sex. When I began to menstruate, when I got my first period, I had no idea of what was happening to me. When she at last understood what had occurred, Grandmother put me to bed, and told me not to take a bath or do exercise, or to work in the kitchen or the garden. She was evidently overdoing it and she knew it, but she enjoyed this power, because she could also write about it. I received most, if not all of my sexual education from books and from friends.

Q. Why do you think this happened?

A. One of the negative things about growing up in Buber's house was that there was a generation gap. Grandmother raised us as if sex did not exist. She wrote books in which there was love, even unconventional love. She was also acquainted with persons who lived unconventional private lives. But all this was not expressed in our sexual education, which was virtually nil. And Buber, as I said, kept in the background and did not interfere, or perhaps even know what was going on.

Q. Did you receive physical education?

A. We belonged to a sport club, and we were taught to ski by a private teacher. But, as I mentioned already, all these activities were taken care of by Grandmother. The only sport I remember Buber enjoying was hiking in mountains.

Q. From my research I learned that Buber lived with Paula for quite a few years before marrying her, and their two children were born while they were unmarried. Do you know the entire story?

A. Paula was a Catholic and Buber was a citizen of Austria, where there were no civil marriages. In 1898 when they met, and decided to live together, they had a problem. After seven years Paula was converted to Judaism by an Orthodox rabbi. They were not enthused about the conversion, although Paula was far from being an orthodox Catholic. Later, when asked

about her religion, she would reply: "I'm a pagan."
She grew up in a Catholic home, but never took
Christianity seriously.

Q. What was her relationship to Judaism?

A. No normal intelligent person wants to convert to a
religion whose dogma one doesn't intend to fulfill.
Paula converted without intending to fulfill all the
Mizvoth. But she was a Zionist when she met Buber,
and contributed to the Zionist cause even as a young
woman. She was interested in Judaism before she met
Buber. It did not bother her that the children received
a Jewish and a Zionist education. She helped Buber
write his first two books of Hasidic tales, especially
the book on Rabbi Nachman. When Grandfather
wanted to keep Jewish holidays she helped him willingly, and did everything with German correctness,
including the Passover Seder, Hanukah, Purim and
other holidays. I already mentioned that when Buber
wanted to have a Friday evening service at home she
helped him willingly. From the age of eight we learned
Hebrew, and she accepted that. We always had Hebrew teachers, and when we came to Israel we could
already read the newspaper without problems.

Q. Tell me a bit about the relations between Buber and
Paula.

A. Well, they lived together for more than sixty years—
Paula was twenty when they met and she died at the
age of eighty-one—that is a long relationship to tell
about. Paula was very actively involved in Buber's
work, especially in his choice of words and linguistic
formulations. During mealtimes many of the arguments were about language, especially during the
many years that Buber was translating the Bible. She

took his work very seriously and respected it greatly. She always asked us to be quiet, so as not to interfere with his work. Even though she had a study of her own, she saw his talent as greater than hers. But at times it did peeve her always to give up her own time and energy and dedicate it to his development. Then she would burst out bitterly and angrily.

Q. Did Buber help Paula?

A. At times. For instance, she liked to have the house organized tip-top, and in Israel it didn't come easily. She also didn't learn Hebrew. She was unhappy about her entire situation. Then he tried to encourage her. He also encouraged her to continue her own writing. When she returned to her writing in Israel, far from her friends, readers, and colleagues, he was very happy, and even helped her with the index of the book. He also commented on the fact that in this new book too many people had similar names. . . Perhaps he felt guilty that he had somewhat interfered with her literary career. But to get back to their relations, they almost never parted during these sixty-one years, even for short periods. When they were younger, there were periods of tension, since he studied in Berlin and she lived with the children in Austria. That was when he was still getting a monthly stipend from his father.

Q. Did Paula help Buber create his image, his pose?

A. She was ambivalent. On the one hand she contributed to his pose, and acknowledged and appreciated that he was very talented and worked very hard. She viewed him as someone who has something important to say to the world. And she wanted him to have the opportunity to say it. On the other hand, she would at times speak out and answer him. Once when Buber scolded me for not finishing my Master's thesis, she yelled back at him: "And don't you remember that when you were in the same situation, you read only English novels?" Thus, every so often she would attack his pose. She did not like it when they tried to make him into a prophet. But when he was greatly honored in Germany and the U.S.A., toward the end of his life, she enjoyed it very much. She didn't like to be called "the professor's wife." Perhaps the reason she wrote her books under a different name, a pseudonym, was that she didn't want to be identified as Buber's wife.

Q. Professor Ernst Simon once said that living with Buber was a burden for one's entire life. Would you agree with that statement?

A. My father suffered from it. It was hard to be the son of someone who at the age of thirty was already a Jewish leader and a known philosopher. Why, when Buber reached the age of fifty they had already published a biography of his life. When my father was a teenager, the name of Buber was surrounded by glory, and that made life difficult for him, very difficult. Once he went to a summer camp, and since everyone was asking him whether he was Buber's son, he wrote a big sign with the word "Yes" on it and paraded it around. He felt as if he always was required to behave in a certain manner—be clever, be interested in philosophy. I don't think that it bothered my sister and myself. Buber's fame was sort of distant from us, and we could digest it.

Q. What is the story about Buber's moving from Germany to Israel?

A. From what I know, he first visited Israel in the 1920s—when the Hebrew University was established, and then again in 1934. He was invited to become a professor at the Hebrew University, and the area he was supposed to teach was comparative religion. But orthodox Jews, members of the board of trustees of the university, were against his being professor in this area. They then tried to find him a chair in another area, and they finally decided on anthropology of civilization.

Q. Did Buber receive much money from his father's estate?

A. I don't know. I know that we received the message that his father had died, and Buber flew to Poland for the funeral. He inherited one-third of his father's wealth, which was quite a bit—I don't know how much—but the government of Poland did not allow the money to leave the country, and it remained in a closed bank account.

Q. Did Buber bring much of his wealth with him when he moved to Israel?

A. Again, I don't know many details. When we left Germany, any Jew who left Germany had to leave half of his wealth in taxes. This law was passed after a Jew called Grünspan had killed a secretary to the German embassy in Paris. When he decided to leave, Buber was willing to leave his wealth in Poland to the Germans. At first they rejected his proposal. At last, they agreed to a compromise. Buber would not sell the house in Heppenheim and would return every year for a few months to teach adults in Frankfurt. We came to Israel in 1937, signed up for school, rented an apartment, and returned to Germany. We came back to Israel in the spring of 1938. That was when a lot of the furniture and the books were transferred to Is-

rael. But the house in Heppenheim was not sold. Buber traveled back to Germany in the summer of 1939;
but when he got to Switzerland he was warned not to
dare cross the border into Germany. He then returned
to Israel.

First Interview with Barbara Goldschmidt

(Martin Buber's Granddaughter)

Q. What are your first memories of life with your grandparents?

A. Many of my earliest memories are linked to Buber and Paula, since even before I moved in with them permanently at the age of five, as a result of my parents' divorce, I often lived with them for long periods. I remember a large nice house with a great garden surrounding it, and the permanent demand that I not interfere with Grandfather's work. I don't believe that little children interested Buber very much. He started being interested in children as they grew older.

Q. After you moved in permanently with your grandparents, was Buber in any way involved in your education?

A. As far as I remember he wasn't. Our education was Grandmother's responsibility.

Q. Did he every play with you?

A. No.

Q. When you grew older, did he ever play with you?

A. Not as a spontaneous activity. At times Grandmother would organize an evening of games in which everyone in the household would participate and perhaps a guest or two. Then my sister and I would sit together with the grownups and play games like Monopoly. The two house servants would participate and also Grandfather's secretary. And Buber would be very entertaining. But these evenings were planned ahead; Grandmother would buy prizes for everyone, etc. They were not spontaneous.

Q. Did Buber ever participate in games that demanded physical exertion?

A. Not *my* grandfather. Definitely not. At times Grandmother would try and get him out of the house. She would tell him that she needed help in the garden, pruning or some similar task. But getting him out to do it was difficult, even though she gave him the pruning scissors and showed him what to do. Buber very reluctantly left his study. Only when he went on hiking trips did he do something physical. In his later years he often suffered from health problems that were a result of his always sitting at a desk.

Q. When you were a child, did Buber ever tell you stories before you fell asleep?

A. Never. That was Grandmother's job. She once promised to tell us one thousand different stories, and she held that she fulfilled her promise. She took many of them from folk legends she knew.

Q. Buber never told you stories?

A. Later when we were older and Buber decided that he should make sure that we receive an appropriate Jewish education he would read us a Hasidic story after every Friday evening Sabbath meal. Some were his stories, some were not. We were younger than ten years old and it continued for quite a while, so that we learned quite a bit from his storytelling.

Q. Did Buber participate in family occasions, such as birthday parties?

A. Only in a passive manner. He was more active on our summer hikes.

Q. Did Buber ever help you get dressed as a child, comb your hair, etc.?

A. Never. He hardly took care of himself in these areas, and Grandmother would put out the shirt he would wear.

Q. Any physical interaction with him?

A. Only a kiss when we would depart for someplace or come home from a trip.

Q. Could you approach Buber spontaneously?

A. Hardly ever.

Q. Did he help you with your homework?

A. When we came to ask him something about our studies of the Bible or of Hebrew. We were taught Hebrew and the Bible from an early age by private teachers. This learning was quite intensive.

Q. Was this because Buber knew that he would one day take you to Israel?

A. It was always part of the plan for the future.

Q. Why didn't Paula learn Hebrew?

A. It probably was difficult for her. She didn't have the talent for languages that Buber had. She only knew French and Spanish. When she came to Israel she was sixty years old, and all her friends spoke German or Yiddish, so she gave up on learning Hebrew.

Q. Did Buber express interest in your homework?

A. He only said: If you have problems, come to me.

Q. Did he examine your report cards?

A. Of course he did! We showed our report cards to Grandmother too, but Buber was the one in charge of preaching to us if something was not in order.

Q. Was he concerned about the friends that you brought home?

A. No. That was Grandmother's role. She gave us freedom to choose our girlfriends—we were only allowed to have girls as friends until our mid or late teens. In the summer of 1936 when it was already dangerous for Jewish children to go to summer camp, we set up a mini-camp in our own back yard and invited four of our girlfriends to live with us for an extended period. We set up a tent in the garden.

Q. Did Buber ever discuss with you the reason you grew up in his house?

A. Not really. He left it open. We knew that our parents had been divorced.

Q. Later in life?

A. No, my parents' divorce was not discussed.

Q. When your father went to live in Kibbutz Geva, did your grandfather ever mention the possibility that you live with your father?

A. No, the possibility that we move in with my father was not discussed. We would go to visit him on vacations, but there was always an excuse for our continuing to live with Buber and Paula.

Q. Did your father attempt to take you to live with him?

A. I don't think so. He was willing to yield to his parents' pressure. My mother struggled for us.

Q. How did Paula and Buber relate to your mother after the divorce and the lawsuit?

A. They accepted her very well. They encouraged us to save money from our allowance so that we could buy presents for Mother. She would come and live in our house for a few days when she visited us, and felt pretty comfortable with the situation.

Q. I understand you were parted from her for many years?

A. Yes, when Hitler came to power she fled the country because she was a communist. She then went to the Soviet Union and spent time in concentration camps. We didn't see her again until after the Second World War.

Q. When did you see her the last time as a child?

A. She fled Germany to Switzerland in 1934 and lived there with a false passport. She wrote to us under a false name to come visit her. Buber and Paula had to identify the handwriting, since she had signed her false

name. We—all of us, Buber, Paula, Judith, and myself—took off immediately for Switzerland and spent
two days with mother. It was in the middle of the
school year, but Buber and Paula considered it important enough to drop everything and go.

Q. Did Buber ever talk to you as a child about your parents' divorce?

A. Never. Only Grandmother spoke about it when we
were older. And then she gave us her version of the
story.

Q. So Buber and Paula and not your parents were your
main educators?

A. Yes, my father would come and take us on trips; once
there was talk about Judith going to live with them,
but it all faded and we grew up with Buber and Paula.

Q. What was Raphael's relation to his father?

A. There was a great deal of tension. Now, Raphael has
read much of Buber's writings and has a definite view
about them. But when he was younger it was very
difficult for him. He suffered because they didn't send
him to school, but tutored him privately. It was convenient for them because it didn't tie Buber and Paula
to any specific place or school schedule. At the age of
12 Raphael was sent to high school and Buber demanded that he bring home high grades. But private
tutors had not prepared Raphael for school, even
though his parents thought that they knew more than
most teachers. I experienced similar frustrations when
I went to school in the third grade after having been
tutored for two years.

Q. How did Buber live so affluently as a free-lance writer
and editor? Was that his major source of income?

A. I don't think so. I believe that most of the money
came from Poland, where his rich father lived and had

large estates, property and investments. As far as I remember, when money stopped coming from Poland, Buber felt the pinch, despite his fame and even though he had other sources of income—his writings and lectures. Yes, most of his wealth was inherited.

Q. Was Raphael angry at Buber for the type of education that he received?

A. He indicates that it was difficult, because when he didn't get good grades there was trouble.

Q. I understand that in the middle of his high school studies he left school and joined the Austrian army.

A. True. It was during the First World War in 1917. All the young teachers in school had gone to the army and only the old and sick ones remained. There was one old teacher that kept cursing his students: "Our boys are at the front and you are sitting here spending your time on foolish endeavors. Go join the army." Then at the age of seventeen he decided one day to go join the army. He was sick of hearing all that preaching.

Q. How did Buber respond?

A. I don't know. But they ordered a uniform for him, and later were proud of him.

Q. Did Buber ever speak of the tension between Raphael and himself?

A. No, it was more Paula who would mention it when she was angry. . . .

Q. How were their relations with their daughter, Eve?

A. I think they were quieter. With their own children they were very domineering; with us it was different. I remember Grandmother saying: "Now I understand many things that I didn't understand when your father was young, for instance, that it is natural for a boy to be mischievous."

Q. What was Buber's role in your father's upbringing?

A. I think he was more involved than in our education. Mostly in a negative manner, demanding from Raphael and telling him off when he was out of order.

Q. Did he ever hit Raphael?

A. Sure. My father well remembers being slapped in the face by his father.

Q. Did Paula succeed as an author, did she feel she had succeeded?

A. She wasn't a great success, but she wrote a few books. Some of them were rather successful when they appeared. At least one I remember. She was proud that the first down payment for the house in Talbiyah came from this book.

Q. How would you define the relationship between Buber and Paula?

A. It was a very strong relationship. Buber and Paula were very dependent upon each other—mutually dependent. They had a very clear division of roles between them.

Q. How was she dependent upon him?

A. Money. She was not the person who brought in the money. She did not come from a rich home. Her home was middle class, but not affluent. And she left home at a young age.

Q. Did her parents assist her when she was young?

A. Paula's parents died when she was young, and she had no connections to her family.

Q. Do you think that Buber and Paula played the role of mother and father to each other?

A. I don't think so. Buber was raised in a warm home by his grandparents.

Q. How does Eve feel today about her parents? How does she talk about them?

A. She still hasn't forgiven them the fact that they never sent her to school.

Q. What else?

A. She says she had a pleasant childhood with many nice experiences.

Q. Was Buber involved in these experiences, as a father?

A. He was usually closed in his study. Only on vacations, as with us, would he open up and be more of a family person.

Q. Judith told us that even on the top of the Dolomites he would do proofreading of his Bible translation. Do you remember that, too?

A. Of course, wherever he went he took proofs along with him. He didn't know how to play in nature. He grew up as a *Wunderkind*. Even as a child he didn't know how to play. He was never a normal child, his grandmother spoiled him. She would tie his shoes when he was already in his teens, and would help him put on his suit.

Q. In which other areas was Paula dependent upon Buber?

A. In Israel her situation was difficult. She came at the age of 61 and never got used to living here, and she lived here for twenty years. She was interested in her neighbors, but hardly ever went out of her house. We would take her shopping at times, but not much more. She had a feeling that with German she would not get around.

Q. When guests came, would Buber invite her to participate in the discussion?

A. As hostess she was in charge of welcoming the guests. But in later years she fled from this duty. She would go to rest. Only when a couple would come to visit would she feel obligated to act as hostess.

Q. Why did you decide to live with Paula and Buber after the Israeli War of Independence? Was it in order to help them? I understand that you, your husband, and your family lived with Buber and Paula for quite a few years.

A. There was also an economic reason. My husband had been sick for almost a year in a hospital in Jerusalem, while I lived and worked in Haifa. We decided to move to Jerusalem. In 1946 Buber and Paula decided to spend some time abroad, and asked us to live in their house and take care of it while they were out of the country. We did not have children yet, so when they returned we rented a room and lived there until 1948. Our room was in an Arab neighborhood, and when the War of Independence broke out we were advised by the Israeli army to get out of that neighborhood. We lived with friends for a while and had no permanent place. Similarly, Buber and Paula had to abandon their house in an Arab neighborhood. It was a beautiful house with a view of the Dead Sea. They wanted to stay there but were cut off from Jewish Jerusalem, until their only link was by phone. They finally left and their landlord—an Arab—promised to take care of their things, which he did. The Anglican Bishop came to their home in a car, and took them with their few suitcases to a hotel in Jewish Jerusalem, in Rechaviah. They lived there for half a year until the Israeli army captured some Arab neighborhoods and gave houses to persons who had been evacuated from other Arab neighborhoods. In the meantime, an Arab teacher lived in Buber's old house and took care of Buber's furniture and books. Once he was under fire and couldn't go out to buy food, but the telephone still worked, so he called Buber and

Paula and asked if he and his family could eat some of the food they had left. They agreed.

Q. Was it after all this that you started living with Buber and Paula?

A. Oh, yes, to get back to that, Buber received this house from the neighborhood committee in Talbiyah, but only if he would live in it together with another family. By the way, the Arab teacher who lived in Buber's former house once sent us regards from Amman.

Q. Why did the newspapers say that Buber, who preached Jewish-Arab dialogue, was living in a house that was forcefully taken from Arabs?

A. What the newspapers said was true, and the former owner of this house once dropped in to see it. But when he received this house Buber himself was a refugee, he had to abandon his own house. When we came to visit Buber at the hotel one day, they suggested that we move in together into this house, so they could get it from the neighborhood committee. It was important to decide quickly, since Buber's library lay in meal sacks scattered around in different places. We also felt that we needed a place of our own, so we agreed. As it later turned out, we could thus help Buber and Paula when they grew older.

Q. Why is it called Buber's house? It's also your house.

A. Yes, but it was Buber who paid the rent and the utilities and fixed it up in those years.

Q. Do you have anything to add concerning Paula's dependency upon Buber?

A. She never went anyplace alone after she came to Israel.

Q. What were Buber's relations with people who worked for him? For instance, his last secretary, Margot Cohen. To us she seemed over-discreet.

A. It's hard to answer. She seems to be a discreet person.

Margot and Buber seldom spoke about personal matters. She started to work for him when Grandmother passed away. He would employ secretarial help from time to time, but usually for very simple jobs, technical jobs like putting the library in order. Margot Cohen got started with these kinds of jobs and slowly became involved in much more difficult undertakings. She seems to regard any word that is not relevant to Buber's work or writings as a family secret; she also believes that secretaries should keep quiet.

Q. And finally, was Buber an open person?

A. He was open to people who came to consult him about their problems and to ask him about problems on an intellectual level. With us and with Raphael he was much less open, perhaps because he was open to others.

Q. Did he ever discuss his own personal problems with you?

A. Only when I started taking care of him after Grandmother died.

Q. Did he every say to you: Look, many people come to me with their problems, why hasn't it happened in my own family?

A. I don't believe he was conscious of what was happening; neither was I. . . . Now in perspective I can see that often our relations with Buber were much less open than normal relations between parents and children.

Second Interview with Barbara Goldschmidt

Q. Have you read Buber's writings?

A. Many of them. But I never read them systematically. I read what interested me. I didn't read them in order to write a paper. I don't remember his more philosophical writings that well.

Q. Since you lived so long with Buber, can you tell about some incidents in which he impressed you?

A. One impressive incident occurred one day when Buber was already very old and was sick with a high temperature, and a group of young people from various countries was supposed to come visit him that day. I suggested that he cancel the meeting. He answered: "No, I have to do it, I must meet with them and converse with them." I asked him how many would come, and he answered that he didn't know, perhaps nobody. Thirty people came that afternoon, people from all races, from Europe, Africa, and the Far East, and it was really crowded in his study. They had a guide who was also a translator. Since they spoke three or four different languages they arranged that people would translate the answers and the questions into all the languages. After a few moments Grandfather took it all into his own hands. He would translate the question into the other languages by himself and then answer the question in the three or four languages that they spoke. Even though most of the questions were not profound and dealt with elementary theology, he handled all the translations like an acrobat. I called some neighbors to see him doing this and they stood outside the windows for over an hour and watched with fascination. Remember, he did all this while he was running a high fever.

Q. Do you remember another incident where he impressed you?

A. It is interesting that mainly events from his last years come to mind. I remember going with him to Amsterdam to receive the Erasmus prize. That was a few years before he passed away and Buber was already partially blind. He gave one lecture to all the dignitaries and professors of philosophy and theology. The lecture was prepared beforehand and Buber had it typed up in especially large letters so he could read it. The lecture was brilliant. Afterward they asked him to speak the next day with representatives from the Zionist Movement together with some people from the university. There he spoke freely and was even better than the day before. Afterward, there was a dinner for all the dignitaries and the princess came, and Buber sat and joked with the princess for a long time.

Q. Were there times when Buber argued with you?

A. Of course. At times we had vicious arguments, especially about political matters. And there were times when he got so angry that he would leave the room and slam the door behind him.

Q. Was Buber an authoritative person?

A. Very. For instance, in this house that we lived in together, he was the central person in the household and left no doubt in anybody's mind that he was in charge.

Q. How was this authoritativeness expressed?

A. For instance, the children were always warned to keep quiet so as not to interfere with Buber. We took our meals together, with him presiding.

Q. Do you find yourself similar to Buber in anything?

A. Me? Not all all! In our family there were always practical persons side by side with intellectuals. I belong to the practical side of the family.

Q. What sort of friendships did Buber establish?

A. When we were children he had some friends who were not necessarily interested in Buber's intellectual contributions. We would, at times, go for walks together with a psychiatrist and his family. But later all the persons who came to visit Buber were interested in his thought. We did not sit together with Buber's friends and socialize. They came, sat in his study, with him behind the desk, and discussed problems. Grandmother was partially to blame since she distanced him from everyday events for sixty years.

Q. What kind of everyday events?

A. The little things that arise in every household—she made sure that these little things never interfered with what Buber had to do.

Q. What kind of people came to meet with Buber?

A. Admirers of all kinds. Many of them soon learned that meeting with Buber was not necessarily a spiritual encounter. Others came because they had intellectual interests that they shared with Buber.

Q. Do you have anything to add concerning the relationship between Buber and Paula?

A. Yes, I don't think that I mentioned that she was his stylistic editor. Buber's style was a rather heavy German, at times overly emotional, and Grandmother would often correct his style. He consulted her in all his writings and explained all his ideas to her.

Q. Did Buber ever write in Hebrew?

A. Very seldom. I remember that when he came to Israel at the age of Sixty he had to write up the lectures that he planned to give at the Hebrew University, because he was not yet comfortable with lecturing in Hebrew. In German and in other languages he could lecture freely; with Hebrew he had problems.

First Interview with Chava Strauss

(Martin Buber's Daughter)

Q. We are interested in your relations with your father and mother.

A. I was born in 1901 and was close to my parents for many years. Only in 1935, at the age of 34, when my husband and I and our two sons left Germany for Israel, did I separate from my parents for a length of time. They came to Israel in 1938. Before leaving for Israel we stayed in their home in Heppenheim for about three months. Father was lecturing in Berlin for a while and then Father and Mother traveled to Israel for two months. We had to stay in their house because Father received a lot of mail, and he wanted someone to be in the house because of the hostility of the Nazis. While they were away, a detective came to examine the house.

Q. What kind of education did you receive?

A. I did not go to school. I think that my parents made a mistake in not sending me to school. We were then citizens of Austria living in Germany, and the law required all German citizens to send their children to school. It did not require Austrian citizens to do that. Father and Mother told me that they feared I would suffer at school because I was sensitive. I did go to school for a short period when I was six or seven, but they withdrew me. I didn't especially enjoy school, but I definitely didn't suffer there. My parents found it convenient for me and my brother not to be in school. Then they were not tied down to one specific place or to the school calendar. They liked to travel, in general, and went to Italy almost every summer. I loved Italy and the beaches there. Mother would rent a house for us for the season. It was there that she employed an Italian maid who stayed with us for twenty years.

Q. What did Buber teach you?

A. Mother taught me reading and writing and in the beginning she also taught me mathematics. When I grew a bit older I studied history with Father. I had a private teacher who taught me French. There was a free school near Heppenheim and Mother had good relations with the school staff, and every week I'd receive a French lesson there from a teacher whom I liked very much. When I advanced in mathematics, one of my parents' uncles, who was a math professor, would at times come to Heppenheim to teach me mathematics. That was when I was 15 years old; until then Mother taught me. At that age I would also have conversations with Father on spiritual topics; he would clarify concepts, define them. It was an exercise in philosophy. When I was around sixteen, Father read the first draft of *I and Thou* with me and it influenced my entire life, including my relationship to religion. I always tried to live in light of the book's message.

Q. So when you grew older your mother taught you less?

A. Mother taught me literature. Many of the other subjects were taught by Father.

Q. Did you receive a religious education?

A. Yes, mainly through the reading of the Bible. Father read the Bible frequently with Raphael and me. When Raphael left home, Father continued to read the Bible with me.

Q. What was the level of your education? Would you say that it was comparable to the German Gymnasium?

A. No. It was basic, and I don't think that it was a sufficient education, even though learning was interesting. My brother did go to high school, but then left it to enlist in the Austrian army. I had private teachers for English and French, I read Shakespeare in English and loved my French teacher. I spoke and understood Italian, since we spent a lot of time in Italy. When I was four, we spent three-quarters of a year in Florence. And we also had an Italian maid. I learned geography, physics and chemistry from my parents; at times Mother, at times Father taught me. I learned many humanistic subjects. Basically, I was taught every day at set hours. I was sorry that I didn't go to school, but I liked my parents' tutoring and I can see the good sides of it—I received lessons that schools don't give. I was sorry about it when I was a young girl, but I didn't suffer. I had friends. My husband suffered in school, and perhaps I suffered a bit by not going to school.

Q. Did you have friends?

A. Sure, I had friends in the street where we lived in Berlin; also Gustav Landauer's daughter was a close friend. When we moved to Heppenheim I joined the youth movement *Blau and Weiss* [Blue and White], which was a Jewish youth movement.

Q. What sort of activities went on in that youth movement?

A. We had a meeting place close to Heppenheim where we'd have meetings on topics that the counselor brought up. I felt close to her. We also went hiking and visited places like Mannheim. There were times when all the members of my *Blau and Weiss* group came to visit me and stayed over in our house. The youth movement had good relations with my father and mother. All the members of this youth movement went to school except me, and I probably was sad about it, but I don't think that I suffered. When I grew older I saw the positive aspects of learning at home; perhaps now that I've reached old age I see more positive aspects. I think the main reason my parents did it was that it was to their personal benefit; they were not tied down to my getting an education.

Q. What about continuing your education when you grew up?

A. I did go to a school when I was 18 years old. It was a gardening school; gardening then attracted me as a possible profession. Later I wanted to continue my studies in this field in Stuttgart, but my parents were against it.

Q. What happened?

A. Father spoke with me and influenced me to give up the idea. He said that a person has to be in a certain place and to have influence in that place. He added that Mother needed me then and that was the place where I should be and strive to have an impact. I believe that Father was right when he said that each person must try and be in the right place to make a mark, and this statement has accompanied me my entire life. I felt that many times I lived according to this statement. But in that specific instance my father was wrong. A young woman should leave her home and learn outside of home. It was Father's mistake; Mother influenced Father and it was his mistake. A young person should learn to live outside of home, and then do what Father said.

Q. Did you continue your studies elsewhere?

A. Only as an auditing student. You see, since I learned at home I did not matriculate, and could not be accepted at a university. From Heppenheim I would travel to Heidelberg, which is not far off, and audit lectures there, mainly literature and other general topics. I wanted to learn to work with abandoned children at an institute for abandoned children in Freiburg. Again my parents were against it, for the same reason—they wanted me to stay at home. At home I did some gardening in our large garden, practicing what I had studied. We had a great garden in Heppenheim, even Father worked there at times.

Q. So, your parents did not allow you to develop a vocation?

A. No, they didn't. They just didn't want me to leave home. My vocation, which was to work with problematic children, came much later, after I was married and we were living in Israel. I took some courses in psychology as an auditor at the Hebrew University, and began working, under the guidance of the psychology professor, with problematic children.

Q. What did you mean when you said that you lived according to the statement that you were always in the right place?

A. I felt that way when I was working with problematic children, when I was taking care of my sick husband, even when Mother passed away in Venice, I was there, since I had come to Venice to meet my parents and to spend my vacation with them. Mother became ill and we took her to a hospital at the Lido where she passed away. I was there at the right time, in the right place.

Q. And the education you didn't get, how do you feel about that?

A. Today I think it would have been better if I had studied in a much more serious manner, had gone to the university and received a degree in psychology, and then worked with problematic children. But I can't say now that I'm very sorry that it didn't turn out that way.

Q. What were your relations with your father after your mother's death?

A. Father felt very bad and wanted me to come live with him, which I did, for about a year, in Barbara's house. But then Barbara thought that there was no need for me to stay there, since she had to live all the time with my parents. I thought she was right and I left. But I was in constant contact with Father and traveled with him to Germany when he went to lecture, or to conferences. Later I traveled with him to Paris, to Switzerland, and to Florence.

Q. Let's go back to your childhood. What parts of your education did you father take upon himself?

A. When we were young children, most of the education was in Mother's hands, and we had little relationship with Father. Taking care of us, washing us, combing us, all that was Mother's job. She alone educated us in those years. When we reached the age of seven or eight, Father started getting involved in our education. But when we were younger it was Mother who educated us.

Q. Did Buber ever play with you, take you for a walk, beat you?

A. Father beat me once—really hard. I told Mother a secret, something intimate, and she wanted to tell it to others. I told her that it was a secret and she shouldn't tell but she ignored me. I got so angry that I grabbed her and started yelling at her. Then Father came out of his study and beat me very hard. Strong smacks. I was about ten years old then. After I quieted down I thought about it and entered his study and told him the entire story about Mother's behavior and told him that he had made a mistake in hitting me before hearing my side. He told me that he was sorry, and that the beating would stand to my credit, so the next time I was wrong he wouldn't beat me. But I was a good girl and never had the chance to use the credit. And I enjoyed hearing him say that he was sorry. During vacations we would go on hikes, but we mainly hiked with Mother. On vacations he would not work in his study; we would go to the mountains.

Q. Did Buber supervise your studies and your achievements?

A. Yes, yes. Mother, too. But I must say that I had an inferiority complex when I compared myself to Mother or to Father. They were great personalities, and I didn't feel that I was. But once Father told me that every person should be satisfied with what he received, and after that I felt better. I believe that when I was young I received warmth and motherly love from my Mother. But the major influence on my life came from Father. I should add, though, that I did not overcome the feeling of inferiority and become more secure as a person until after I married and received a feeling of security from my late husband. I don't want to blame my parents, I'm not a great personality like they were, and I did get some support from what Father told me then.

Q. How were your relations with the servants?

A. Excellent. We would play with them at times. One maid lived with us for twenty years. In general, the entire atmosphere was of a patriarchal family. Mother organized it that way, with the servants as part of the family.

Q. While you were growing up, did Buber share with

you some of the thoughts he was having about what was going on—for instance, his response to the First World War?

A. Not really. Later I learned that at first Buber was a patriot and wholeheartedly supported the war and that Landauer was against the war and criticized Buber's chauvinism. But I learned about these discussions from Landauer's daughter. Later Father told me that he had had a problem when he was young—he lived too much in the realm of spirit or of intellect. In that period he did not live according to the spirit of his later writings, where the relations between person and person are very important. Later he endeavored to work against this trend of living too much in the realm of the mind.

Q. What was your parents' response when Raphael enlisted in the Austrian army?

A. They were unhappy about it. He went when there was no longer any need, toward the end of the war. They didn't tell him not to go, but they weren't happy when he went. At first Father was very patriotic and that might have influenced Raphael. Later, though, they were not supportive of the war efforts. Once, when Raphael and I went to a party supporting the war, they were not happy about our being with all those chauvinists.

Q. Do you know why Paula and Buber had only two children?

A. I believe they didn't want more children, but it was never a topic they discussed with us.

Q. How were your relations with Raphael as a child?

A. Good. Very good. Of course, at times he would hit me, but in general he acted like a good big brother. If someone in the street would try and hit me he always came to my defense. If I had problems he always helped me. He was stronger than I was, but we would play together. When we were very young, we slept in the same room, and then we had a world of imagination that we shared together. We never told anyone about it. These good relations continued our entire life, and even now he is in charge of the estate and helps me with that. When my husband died he was a great support. He took me to his home in Haifa, and when I would cry he would hug me. His wife supported me also.

Q. How were your relations with your parents after you left home and got married?

A. Good. In Germany we would sometimes visit them at Heppenheim and then they would play with their grandchildren. Father had a warm relation with his grandchildren. He was interested in them when they were much younger than when he first started taking in interest in Raphael and myself. Only when we grew up did Father establish a relationship with us. But with his grandchildren it was much earlier.

Q. What were the relations between Buber and Paula?

A. I can't imagine them not together. Mother helped him a lot in his work. He asked her everything, and after Mother passed away I felt that he wanted me to do the same. In all his work he consulted her, and when he translated the Bible she was in charge of helping him with language.

Second Interview with Chava Strauss

Q. We'd like to concentrate mainly on what you remember Buber telling you about his childhood, beyond his published recollections. For instance, how did Buber speak about his parents' divorce, or his life at his grandparents?

A. He hardly ever mentioned his parents' divorce. He did speak warmly of the period when he lived with his grandparents; he lived with them from the age of three to fourteen, after his mother eloped with her lover.

Q. What about his schooling?

A. Until the age of ten he studied at home with tutors; he mainly learned languages—he was talented in this field. When he went to school he had friends. He did say that as a child he would play in his mind with different languages. In his mind he had a game where he directed a play in which the two heroes of the play were different languages. He thought about languages a lot during his childhood.

Q. What happened when Buber went to live with his father?

A. I think that he appreciated his father, but that he received love mainly from his grandmother.

Q. Was Buber active politically as a youth—say, in a youth movement?

A. As a youth he wasn't active. During his student years he became active in the Zionist movement.

Q. Was Buber a good pupil at school?

A. Definitely. Learning came very easily to him, always. He would always joke about the fact that he did not start speaking until he was four, but still learned quite a bit during his life.

Q. Was he an adventurous child?

A. He didn't talk about that. He would tell about going for walks with his father in the fields.

Q. Did Buber ever speak about childhood friends?

A. I don't remember him ever speaking about that.

Q. As a child, was Buber ever naughty?

A. My impression is that he wasn't. He was clumsy with his hands and told us that he had had this problem since childhood. He was sorry he hadn't learned to be more dexterous with his hands when he was a child. My mother used to say that since father's grandmother spoiled him when he was a child, she had to continue to pamper him his entire life.

Q. What childhood games did Buber remember?

A. Chess.

Q. Could he ride horseback?

A. I think he told us about riding horseback as a child.

Q. Did he play or participate in any sport or physical game?

A. No. The only physical activity he enjoyed was hiking. He regretted this.

First Interview with Emanuel Strauss

(Martin Buber's Grandson)

Q. What are your first memories of Buber?

A. I was born in 1926 in Aachen, Germany, where my father worked as a lecturer, so we lived rather far away from my grandparents. We visited them on summer vacations, and I think that my first clear memory of them is when my mother and I continued from Heppenheim to Italy together with Buber, Paula, and my cousins, Judith and Barbara. I liked being in Italy. I swam in the sea; I was four years old then. My father joined us a bit later. One night there were fireworks and Barbara and Judith were allowed to go out to see them. My father did not allow me to go out. Then Buber and Paula intervened and said that was not fair; if the girls were out there I should be allowed to go out too. My father agreed and I went out. I still remember those fireworks.

Q. How did Buber relate to you when you visited him?

A. Sometimes he would play with me. One game we played was to have a boxing match. When I would tell him that I'd smear him to the wall, he would laugh. But Grandmother did not like my saying that.

Q. Did you visit him often?

A. We went to Heppenheim once a year, in the summer. We would often go on hikes together. It was nice; there was a large, spacious garden and I'd play a lot with Barbara and Judith. At times Buber would join the games; I remember him playing hide and seek with us. We once visited them for Passover, and I remember them hiding colored eggs in the garden, and we all went out to look for them.

Q. Did Buber keep the Passover Seder?

A. Yes. When we were in Israel he would preside at a family Seder. Later when some of the participants were unhappy with his religious approach he canceled the family Seder. He did not want to impose his views.

Q. What do you remember from your walks in Heppenheim?

A. It's a beautiful area. We would climb the mountain and there was a synagogue there. Buber often joined us on these walks; he was a good hiker. Sometimes we played on these hikes. But Buber also sat a lot in his study.

Q. What sort of atmosphere prevailed in Buber's house?

A. A good atmosphere. There was tension at times, but the tension differed from what I saw in other families. I don't remember Buber raising his voice. He was always temperate. Paula could be sharp.

Q. What happened when you came to Israel?

A. We came in 1935; Buber and Paula came a few years later. We lived much closer to them there and saw them more often. I felt comfortable in their house and would consult with Buber about my problems. When I decided to become an arts and crafts teacher I consulted with him and he encouraged me to do that. He mentioned that he regretted that he hadn't learned to work with his hands when he was young. In short, he encouraged me.

Q. Did Buber express interest in your studies?

A. Yes. He asked about my studies; he would keep the things that I made and brought him. He liked my crafts; at times he even admired them. He did very little work with his hands, even around the house, perhaps because Grandmother did everything.

Q. What happened at the family Seder when Buber led it?

A. We would read the entire Hagaddah, he would inter-
pret sections of it, add stories. He would then buy the
Afikoman in a dramatic way. At times he told stories
that were linked to the exodus from Egypt.

Q. Did he tell stories on other occasions?

A. Infrequently. He read from his Hasidic tales.

Q. Did Buber inquire about the details of your studies?

A. Yes, he was amazed at my ability to make high grades
in arts and crafts and low grades in mathematics.

Q. Did he inquire about your personal problems?

A. At times he would ask a straightforward question like:
"Are you happy with your marriage?" He would look
deep into my eyes to see if the answer was sincere. It
was therefore difficult to lie to him. We viewed him
as a person who had the power of penetrating one's
soul beyond the regular power of a normal person.
Even though he had weaknesses, when he spoke there
was wisdom in what he said. He related to me as if I
was one of his students. There was almost no friction.
He was a paternal figure. I would usually come to him
to get advice, and I was always a bit tense until I heard
what he had to say. I felt the radiance of his personality and felt secure because I had such a grandfather.
When I had problems in school I'd come to him without setting up a meeting, and he would always see
me. At times he would be sunk in thought, but after
a while it would pass.

Q. Did he express concern?

A. Yes. At times he would ask me, "How are you?" I'd
answer, "Fine, thank you." Then he'd say, "No, I really
want to know how you are, tell me in detail." After
that we would talk at length. He never told me, when
I came to him with my problems, "I don't have any
time."

Q. Were you always with him only for short periods, like for vacation or when you wanted to consult him?

A. There was one period when I spent more time with him and Grandmother. In 1944 I joined the Jewish Brigade. After I was released from the British army, in 1946, I lived for a year and a half with Grandfather and Grandmother in their house in Jerusalem. I had no room of my own and I wanted to work as a teacher, and living with them fitted my needs. Also, during the War of Independence, when I was stationed in Jerusalem their apartment was my home. They lived in a hotel in Abu Tur and I would often visit them. Grandmother would wash my uniform for me. During that period I felt close to them. I sensed that they were worried about the situation. They were very interested in what was happening and questioned me about details.

Q. How were the relations between Buber and Paula?

A. They had a good relationship. She was a very demanding woman who often voiced her criticism. She wanted things to get done. If Buber ever demanded something from me, it was because she influenced him to do so. She was a strong person. He was more of an expressive person, while she was more of an instrumental person. He was tolerant. At times he would make demands in order to support her. I think that the relations between them were very good. He loved her deeply and admired her. She admired him, even though she was often aggressive and impulsive. She had a sharp tongue and used it against him and against everyone. Her writing was satiric.

Q. So, as a child you liked to visit them?

A. Yes, it was an important event since they were wealthy, while we were not at all wealthy. Buber treated us like the good grandfather. We waited for these trips; we liked the atmosphere, the feeling that the maids were there to wait on you, the rich meals, the big garden, the bicycles, and also the entire area was enchanting. Even though Grandmother was a tough person, we wanted to come. When we were young children we'd get up early on Saturday and Sunday and steal into their beds. Grandfather and Grandmother liked it, but when we grew older, 8 or 9 years old, we stopped doing it. When we were young, Barbara and Judith would join us in our grandparents' bed, and all of us would have a great time.

Q. Was Buber open as a person?

A. He was open. Whoever called and asked to speak to him was accepted: workers, students, intellectuals. At times Grandmother would guard his time and not let him sit too long with someone. He was not an intimate person who would tell you his own problems. He never was against opposite views. He never tried to impose his own views.

Q. Did he visit your parents at their house?

A. Not often. In Israel more than in Germany. When we lived at a youth school, where my father worked, Buber came and organized a joint Bar Mitzvah for me and for other boys of my age. At times we would write to him. Usually, though, we would go to visit him rather than he and Paula coming to visit us.

Q. Did he criticize your way of life?

A. Grandmother didn't like my not being an orderly person, and she would not forgive me at times like that, but grandfather would only say, "Try more next time." He might ask why it happened that I forgot to do something.

Q. Could you tell a bit more about your visits to Heppenheim as a child?

A. We went to Heppenheim only during school vacations. On Sundays we would go for hikes; there was a fortress above the town that we would walk to and talk along the way. There were joint meals with my parents and grandparents, the granddaughters and my brother and myself. Grandmother was a good cook, and taught the maids to cook well. The meals were sort of celebrations.

Q. And your visits to Buber in Israel?

A. Much the same, except that at times some of Grandfather's friends came for coffee. Agnon was among those who came, and he and Grandfather would tell each other stories and discuss them. I don't remember special topics of discussion. In Heppenheim we would discuss the view as we walked. In Israel, Judith and Barbara would discuss politics with Grandfather and at times they got excited. Buber never got excited.

Q. For how long did Buber organize a Passover Seder for the entire family?

A. Until 1938, I believe; when the granddaughters were 17 or 18 he stopped. Buber would read most of the Haggadah. Chauvinistic sections he would not read, like the section asking God to pour his wrath upon non-Jewish nations. There were sometimes guests, in addition to the immediate family. Buber would also discuss certain passages that were not clear or that he felt were worthy of being discussed. He would sometimes ask us questions to see what we had learned or understood. In Heppenheim the maids would cook; in Israel Grandmother cooked and Barbara and Judith helped bring in the food. After the Seder we would play games.

Q. Did the family get together on other holidays?

A. At times on Hanukkah. We would light the candles, sing some songs, and then play games.

Q. Do you remember any painful incidents that had to do with Buber?

A. I did have one painful experience that had to do with Buber in an indirect manner. I was in a youth movement and the counselor was quite enthusiastic about convincing us to join a kibbutz. I was fifteen years old and kibbutz life didn't excite me. Later the counselor started talking about Arabs and said that there was no way to talk to them and that we must take back the land by force. I disagreed, even though the entire group agreed with him. During the argument I mentioned that I had read something in German. The counselor then and there forbade me to continue reading in German. I said that my grandfather wrote German and he told me to spit in my grandfather's face. Afterward he had to apologize, even though he said he never remembered making that statement. But the entire group remembered. Buber did not get excited about the counselor's statement. But I was hurt by the entire situation. Buber said that it was unfortunate that a counselor would bring parents and grandparents into his arguments.

Q. Do you remember any other personal meetings with Buber in which he helped you or influenced you?

A. When I was in basic training in the British army I had some problems that I shared with grandfather. He listened and suggested how to behave with people. He said not to be hurt by the behavior of some of my commanders, because they were merely doing their job.

Q. When he questioned you was he always straightforward?

A. He would mainly listen carefully when you came to him with a problem and then say, "I can't say how you should respond but only how I would respond." His way of listening gave me a feeling of security. I would feel that there was a solution to the problem.

Q. How did you feel when you lived with your grandparents in 1947?

A. Good. I was a closed person and didn't have many friends. I liked coming home after work, drinking coffee with them and then eating supper. It was always interesting to be with them. They were happy when I brought someone over. I once brought a girlfriend. That happened rarely, though, because, as I mentioned, I was a closed person.

Q. Why was there such a great difference between Buber's standard of living and his daughter's standard of living? Didn't Buber help your family financially?

A. As far as I know Buber was used to a high standard of living and he spent all the money he made as a university professor on his own needs. Sometimes he did help us financially. My father was a public school teacher and did not make much money. At times we would get presents from them.

Q. Was Buber happy with your mother's marriage?

A. I believe he was, since my father got to know my mother while visiting Grandfather. I believe Buber loved my mother; she was very comfortable coming to their home quite frequently. Buber saw it as a good marriage.

Interview with Micha Strauss

(Martin Buber's Grandson)

Q. When did you first get to meet with Buber?

A. As a child when we visited my grandparents in Heppenheim, and later in Israel.

Q. Did Buber play any significant role in your education?

A. I don't think he educated me, but I learned from him through reading his books, and also later through discussions with him. I remember a few interesting philosophical discussions with him.

Q. Were you impressed by Buber?

A. I don't remember any special event at which he impressed me. The Passover Seder for the entire family, at which Buber presided, and the games we played together afterward come to mind.

Q. Do you think that Buber influenced you?

A. I learned from him and was influenced by his views, for instance by his book *Paths in Utopia*. I appreciated his ability to listen to other persons even when he was quite old. His openness impressed me.

Q. How do you remember Buber?

A. I remember him as being, even in his old age, an attentive person who spoke eloquently with an element of drama in his presentation. His listeners were captured by the human element of what he said, his voice, his movements. In his lectures when someone asked him a question he would, at times, come closer to that person, even sit on the arm of the person's chair, while listening. After grandmother died he would sit quite a bit with Barbara, converse with her and discuss problems with an openness that is quite unusual at that age. He was good to me. He helped me financially when I decided to take some time off for research, even though I did not approach him and ask for money. He gave me 1,000 pounds, which at that time was quite a bit of money. He would also bring me books from abroad when he traveled. I remember his fascinating memory for languages and for recalling details. He was capable of being deeply impressed by something that happened; he knew how to describe people vividly and how to tell a colorful story.

PART II

Contemporaries

First Interview with Jochanan Bloch

(A Professor of Jewish Studies at Ben Gurion U.
He entered this field through Buber's encouragement)

Q. How did Buber view himself?

A. Buber viewed himself as an educator, an educator who was both a doctor and a priest.

Q. Are you trying to say that there was little reciprocity in Buber's relations with other people?

A. I don't really know, and I don't even know whether he had true friends. He always kept a distance between himself and the person he met; he always cultivated a pose. I never heard him use an obscenity. He did tell jokes and knew how to be charming. But perhaps in his relations with me there was a problem because of the difference in our ages, almost two generations. He encouraged me personally, and at times with warmth, natural warmth.

Q. Did Buber ever reveal his own personal problems and inclinations?

A. Rarely. But I believe that it might have been difficult for him to do that with me because I had an inferiority complex toward him. And he took it for granted that one should relate to him as a teacher. Authority emanated from his being. For instance, he was not a person you would slap on the back, or even touch spontaneously. He was extremely careful in his eloquence, saying exactly what needed to be said, but not a word more.

Q. Is there anyone you could describe as Buber's friend?

A. I believe that Ewald Wasmuth from Tübingen was a friend of his, but in their letters they cultivated a pose. Buber visited him and lived in his house for a while. His entire relationship with Neima Beer Hoffman was *not* a testimony of what Buber would have defined as friendship. She seems to have been his mistress after his wife died, but Buber did not allow her to visit him in Jerusalem after he returned from Switzerland, where they had spent some time together. She was sweet and not very bright, and Buber may have needed someone like her for a while.

Q. How did you see Buber?

A. He was definitely not a saint, but he was a great person. But there were riddles to this greatness. For instance, I never met his wife, Paula. He kept her, so to say, on the sidelines.

Q. When you met with him, what constituted this greatness?

A. Buber conveyed the feeling that he had accepted a mission, and for that mission he had to project a certain image. Hence, he never revealed himself. Other people fed that image and made it into a pose, but he invited such a response from those persons. He helped people construct their image of his greatness, imperceptibly, by little cues—but he helped.

Q. Do you see any connection between Buber's personality and his philosophy?

A. Both as a person and as a writer, Buber tried to create the impression that he was a representative of classical Judaism. I think that this was a central weakness of his thought, that it assumed a pose, and this pose influenced his personality. He took himself much too seriously, and his thought much too seriously. He was enslaved by phrases that he himself created and tried to schematize, such as the I-Thou. But as I have shown in my book, this schematization disintegrates from within when approached critically.

Q. How did he relate to you personally?

A. Buber related wonderfully toward me. He was the first person I encountered who sincerely tried to encourage me and was very interested in helping me. He agreed to read something that I had written and then invited me to visit him. He saw that I had some talent and sincerely wanted to help me.

Q. Why didn't Buber write an autobiography?

A. I believe that one basic reason is that he had a weak autobiographical memory.

Q. Were all your meetings with Buber serious?

A. No. He had a sense of humor, but he seldom allowed it to emerge.

Second Interview with Jochanan Bloch

Q. Can you give some details on how you got to meet Buber?

A. I got to know Buber during the last ten years of his life. I first met him around 1955. Ernst Simon was the person who introduced me to Buber, by passing on to Buber a manuscript that I had written. Buber then invited me to come to Jerusalem to visit him. The situation was unique, since I was far removed from Buber's opinions and his philosophical work. I was working on conceptual systematic philosophy, and I wrote essays that were close to the Hegelian school of thought. I was then a practicing lawyer in the town of Pardes Hannah, and did the philosophical writing on the side. I was also not religious, and far removed from Jewish thought. There was another problem. I think that Buber knew about it and did not mention it. What I knew about Buber was his political views and involvement. His opposing Jewish retaliation against Arab terrorism, his work in the Jewish-Arab Friendship League, etc. I was situated at the opposite end of the political spectrum; I was a follower of Menachem Begin. Before I met him, Buber seemed to me to be a grotesque person, almost despicable.

Q. Despicable?

A. Yes, I was especially angry at his views during the 1936–39 period of Arab terrorist attacks against Jews. He opposed retaliation, and I was young, and was very annoyed at such views. In any event, I had my reservations, and I suspect that he knew it. I am telling this because I did not come to him as a believer in his way, as a person close to his views who wished to hear his wisdom. I came to him to ask for help in my personal development.

Q. How did he respond?

A. He responded according to his educational views. He made no attempt to impose his views or his approach. He probably read the manuscript that Simon passed on to him and knew that my views were far distant from his. Still, he never suggested that I read any of his writings; he never tried to correct me. Only once, when I was blocked at a dead end, he suddenly yelled at me: Well, we've agreed that this way does not lead to the goal. This was when I was in despair about my work, without knowing how to continue, and his yelling at me helped me get out of that dead end. He helped the way he should have helped.

Q. When did you first read Buber's writings?

A. Not until about four years later. I was surprised at how much the writings spoke to me and helped me. I then asked myself why he never referred me to these writings, and I even wrote to Buber saying: You exaggerated in conforming to your educational principles, you could have referred me to your writings.

Q. What were the prevailing views about Buber's personality among persons who were not his admirers?

A. There were many negative views about his personality. People said he was an egoist, that he was stingy, and unable to engage in genuine dialogue. From my many meetings with Buber, I must say that there was some justification for these views. But I must also say that toward me he revealed his good side, especially during the first period of our acquaintance.

Q. Can you be a bit more specific?

A. He took one of my manuscripts and tried to convince

publishing houses to publish it. He encouraged me, even though I was perhaps over-ambitious. He accepted me as I was, and tried to help, not because he sought another admirer, or to forward his views. All this was to his credit. Let me summarize what happened.

Q. Go ahead.

A. Through Ernst Simon and Martin Buber I was offered a grant to come to Heidelberg and to continue my studies. Later, I transferred to Berlin, and Buber was angry at me for that. But he continued to correspond with me. When I was in Israel, I met with him at least once a year; afterward, when he traveled regularly to Europe, we would meet in Switzerland. His willingness to meet with me regularly is to his credit. Our meetings were at first dedicated to his helping me receive a grant or publish my writings. We never, but never, spoke about political matters.

Q. Were you impressed by Buber?

A. Greatly. His conversations and personality, the way he related to you as a person, his comments, his image—all these greatly impressed me. I was a bit scared of him. He was the sort of patriarchal figure that sort of threatened me. But I liked to visit him. When he was in Europe he would invite me once a month or so, and I would come. We would converse, and I would be encouraged by his interest in me.

Q. Why didn't you start reading his writings until 1959?

A. That was part of a personal complex. But when I did start reading them they helped me greatly. I was in a period of crisis and Buber was at the height of his fame, in Germany and in the entire world. He was famous, his works were being read, but not too extensively. Then I said to myself, let me read some

Buber. I was very impressed and I decided to write my Ph.D. dissertation on Buber and Freud: Dialogue and psychoanalysis. I wrote to him about this decision. From then on during our meetings I tried to learn more details about his thinking, and to encourage him to speak on these topics.

Q. What was Buber's response?

A. He had a good opinion of me, and began to believe that I would bring fame to his theoretical thinking. I believe that he was disappointed in what I wrote about him. The problem was that very little—and nothing serious—had been written about his theoretical thinking. Therefore, he was waiting for my book to appear. The truth was, though, that I could not write my book on Buber as long as Buber was still alive. His greatness threatened me, and the threat was too great for me to sit down and write.

Q. You say that there were no serious studies of Buber's theoretical thinking?

A. I believe that there have been only two major attempts to discuss the implications of Buber's theoretical thinking: the first by Michael Theunissen, the second by myself. When Theunissen completed his book, he sent it with fear and trembling to Buber; but a few weeks later he heard that Buber had died. He then sighed with relief and said: Now many things will be much simpler. After a while I understood Theunissen's response, because I suddenly felt that I too could now write about Buber.

Q. How did Buber encourage your writing about him?

A. He gave me many hours of his time. And he did this even though he did not appreciate psychoanalysis, and in my study I was linking his thought to psychoanalysis. He was often in conflict with psychoanalysis, even though there was something ambivalent about this conflict, since he was close to the therapeutic approach. He rejected analysis because it somewhat competed with his approach. The closeness of psychoanalysis to dialogue was, in his view, dangerous. But, once again, I must say that Buber made no attempt to evade the issue. He did his best to tell me what he could tell. But I must add a point that is well known. Buber was not a dialogical person. He seemed to know the answers and was not open to learning from other persons. His ideas were crystallized and systematized, and he did not budge an inch from these ideas.

Q. Can you give a specific example of this lack of openness?

A. Yes. When Buber was in the United States giving a seminar, he taped a dialogue that he had had about the unconscious. It was then typed up and he thought of publishing it. This happened two or three years before his death. He gave me the manuscript and asked me to go over it and add comments. I took his request very seriously, and also felt proud to undertake such a task. I wrote an addendum in which I attempted to clarify the concepts discussed in the dialogue. It was very difficult, and I was very critical about what Buber had written. Buber received my manuscript and did not respond at all.

Q. What did you do?

A. In the meantime, Buber died before I had the opportunity to discuss all this with him. After he died the essay was published posthumously, and something weird emerged, something that I never would have imagined. Buber published the essay without changing a single word. In other words, all my work was worthless. In addition, it turned out that this was the only essay that he had left without making some changes. Perhaps my criticism led him to leave it as it was. But what I felt was that he had no intention to learn from me. Look, it was well known that in the seminars that Buber gave in America, where students were more open than in Germany, and were willing to argue with him, he was always elusive. They asked him about points that were central to his thinking, and not well clarified—the Eternal Thou, the problems of society, the kibbutz—at times he even got angry during these meetings and refused to respond.

Q. Do you think such responses had anything to do with his age? After all, you were acquainted with Buber when he was in his seventies and eighties.

A. Perhaps. A person of that age does not start making basic revisions in his thought. But my impression was that from the period in which his views on dialogue were formulated—that is, from the 1920s, when he wrote *I and Thou*—since that time Buber had not deviated from his views. He remained faithful to his own position. Perhaps when he was younger he was a bit more open, but in general his position did not change. There might be a psychological reason here. In his youth Buber jumped from one matter to another and worked in many areas, often without much profundity, but with high-flown language. Hence people did not take him too seriously.

Q. Aren't you exaggerating? Even in his youth Buber was perceived as a "rising star." He came to Zionist congresses when he was in his early twenties and spoke there eloquently; he edited *Die Welt*, the Zionist newspaper.

A. He was famous, but the academic and spiritual leaders did not relate to him seriously. They were surprised when in the 1920s he became deeply involved in dialogical thinking. Perhaps Buber believed that by adhering to and developing his dialogical philosophy he had found a way of saving himself from being a passing fad. At last he had found a position that he had formulated. He once told me, "At last I learned to read," and he meant that everything that he read was read in order to justify his own position. One of his most important sayings was: "I have become a sieve." He no longer read because something aroused his interest. Thus, I believe, he closed his mind to experiencing spiritual adventures.

Q. Couldn't you say that Buber merely concentrated his energies on clarifying one realm of human existence?

A. Yes, but this concentration was a blessing for him and saved his name for history. Hence he feared to go beyond those positions that he had formulated and that had brought some blessing to the world. It is good for a person when he finds a clear path; then he doesn't have to take the risk of correcting himself, which often leads nowhere, or is a mixed blessing. He was not very much of a dialogical person, and when he did not want to learn from other persons he did not learn. Ernst Simon once told me: Concerning psychoanalysis Buber is partially blind. That was true. Buber did not want to learn anything about it even though he knew that he was creating a problem for himself.

Q. Was Buber an educator?

A. No! He was definitely *not* an educator. He helped many persons, myself included, and in this his approach was educational. In a narrow area he knew how to support people. But he lacked the basic openness, or the character of openness, that an educator needs. He was really not prepared to do this. He was a writer, a thinker, a scholar with a therapeutic approach—but all these endeavors were based on his own assumptions, which he refused to broaden or abandon. For instance, he was attracted to and worried about the problem of schizophrenia. As a student he worked for a period in a mental hospital. He told me about a person he had known who became schizophrenic and was physically distorted as a result of his illness. Buber played a role in this illness, since the man saw in Buber an imaginary power that was trying to dominate him. The man's wife wanted to help him and emulated his distortions. She became ill also. Buber then tried to help the man and to draw him back to the world. I can almost imagine how he did it. He sat in front of him, looked at him with his large attractive eyes, took off his glasses—Buber never allowed anyone to take his picture while he was wearing glasses—and he spoke to him with his authoritative voice. It had no influence at all. He said so himself. I told Buber: "You should have gone the entire way with this man, you should have descended into his world, his hell. But that is not at all simple; that is the analytic method." Buber answered: "You are right, but I couldn't do it. I have my own field of endeavor." It seemed that his conscience was bothering him. In other words, Buber understood the analytic approach, but found an excuse for his failure in the fact that he was not built for such endeavors. Hence, he was also not built to be an educator.

Q. Do you think that Buber knew this, that he was not an educator?

A. I believe he did. He knew that an educator cannot have a pose, and Buber always cultivated a pose. One incident in which I was personally involved will clarify how deeply the assuming of a pose influenced his entire being: the incident with Neima Beer Hoffmann. Buber got to know her after his wife died, and for a while she was his nurse, when he underwent an operation. But later he fell in love with her and his relations to her were what he would call immediate, intimate, and genuine. In Switzerland they shared an apartment. But here his pose interfered. He himself learned much through his relations with Neima. He was surprised and even struck with wonder at the degree to which his own life was artificial, at least the manner in which he presented himself to the world. But the bitter truth was that his entire environment needed Buber's pose; they had to hold onto it, hence they were extremely angry at the relations that developed with Neima. And as I said in the previous interview, they convinced Buber not to invite her to visit him in Jerusalem. Neima wrote a sad letter to me about this, since during that period my wife and I were frequently with them when Buber was recuperating in Switzerland.

Q. So Buber wrote against assuming a pose, while cultivating one and knowing that he cultivated a pose. Was that pose very central to his life?

A. I believe it was. You see, all the people who surrounded Buber needed his pose too. People didn't like it when Buber was natural or human. For instance, his letters concerning Neima were not published in the three-volume publication of his letters. They are not for the public eye, and I'm not sure that you will be allowed to read them in the Buber archives. Even today there is an attempt to create an image of Buber, an icon of Buber, that is in many respects false. I don't want to open scandals, but this suggests something about Buber's entire approach to life. For instance, he demanded that if his letters be published, they would not include his correspondences with women. It was typical of Buber to make such a decision. And his pose in front of cameras: the man with the beard and the large warm eyes—his desire to always look like this contradicts the principles of dialogue. As he repeatedly pointed out, there is no dialogue between persons who assume a pose. In general, his wanting to be photographed was not a way of reaching out to other persons, since any such picture is ambivalent; it is a way of not being with the other person. No, Buber was not an educator. He was a good person who was prepared to help. He was rigid, perhaps necessarily, and unflexible despite his broad horizons. We must not make of him what he was not.

Q. How did Buber feel as an old man?

A. I believe that he was happy to reach an old age. He once told me: "Bloch, I hope that you will be blessed to live to be an old man." I believe thát he felt great satisfaction at having been able to influence deeply at least two generations, and to see that influence during his lifetime. Today, in Germany, he is back on the sidelines since they are into neo-Marxist thinking, and he is less well known. But when I knew him he could be happy with his life, he could display a sense of humor, and even have romantic adventures at the age of 83 or 84. What is perhaps sad is that his image had more influence than his writings and his work; the period after the Second World War seemed to be waiting for someone like Buber, and he knew how to make use of these expectations. He paid a price for this influence.

Q. How did you accept Buber's death?

A. I have a story to tell about that which somewhat summarizes my relationship to Buber. A few weeks after Buber's death, I met Gershom Scholem's wife in Jerusalem. At times, she was very critical of Buber. While we were standing and talking in the street she told me that Buber had suffered greatly during the week before his death. She added: "Maybe that was a sign from God, making Buber pay for his sins, which were often hidden under his image of a great successor of the Hebrew prophets." I replied: "You know, I'm happy Buber sinned at times." "Why?" She asked. And then I told her the following story:

At the turn of the century, the chief orthodox rabbi of Hungary had a devout son who became involved in Zionist activities. A mutual trust existed between father and son; hence when the father asked: "Why do you spend your time with those who have strayed from the path of Judaism?", the son responded: "Father, come to a Zionist congress, and you will understand." The father agreed to come.

They traveled together to the next Zionist congress in Basel. The son was a delegate and sat in the chamber. The father, an old bearded man with silver sidelocks, sat quietly in the balcony. When the son questioned him a few times as to his impressions, the father was silent. For four full days he sat and listened.

When the congress ended, the father suggested: "Since we have come this far, let us travel a bit farther to Frankfurt, to visit the rabbi there who is a close friend." On the train the father continued to be reticent. The chief rabbi of Hungary was greeted with great honor when the train arrived in Frankfurt. After he had been put up in the house of the local rabbi, and he and his son had rested a bit, they entered their host's study.

"What brings you to our area?" asked the rabbi of Frankfurt.

"We were in Basel," responded the old man.

"And what was your purpose in visiting Basel?"

"We went to the Zionist congress, my son as a delegate, and I merely to listen."

"What?! You went to the Zionist congress! You, the chief rabbi of Hungary! How could you? Why, that Herzl is a nonbeliever. Don't you know that he doesn't eat kosher, that he doesn't pray regularly, that he parades himself without a skullcap, that he doesn't read Hebrew or study the Talmud! How could you go there to listen to such a sinner, to such a perverter of Judaism?"

At last the rabbi from Hungary was compelled to state his impressions. "You are right, Herzl is not an observant Jew," the old man said quietly. "And I thank God for that. I thank God that Herzl doesn't keep kosher and doesn't wear a skullcap or pray. Because if he did, if he were an observant Jew, I would have to climb up to the roof of your house, stand there and proclaim and yell so that all the Jews could hear: The Messiah has come!"

Interview with Aharon Cohen

*(A member of Kibbutz Shaar Haamakim and
a writer on Mideastern topics)*

Q. How did you get to know Buber?

A. In the 1920s in Europe I joined the Hashomer Hatzair
Zionist Youth Movement. At that time Buber's writings on Zionism were a light that illuminated Zionist
education. Buber was also regarded as one of the central thinkers of Zionism. Everyone in the movement
read and studied his three speeches on Judaism. That
was my first meeting with the name Buber.

My first meeting with Buber, the person, occurred
later, in 1939, at a Zionist rally organized to remind
the Zionist movement that it had decided to set up a
board of inquiry on Jewish-Arab relations. From the
end of 1940 on I met with him quite regularly. We
were both members of the Secretariat of the Jewish-
Arab Friendship League, in which we worked together until the end of the British Mandate in 1948.
During this period I was frequently in Jerusalem; I
would meet Buber at meetings and also visit him at
his home. One of the regular times for our meetings
was before the meetings of the Secretariat got started.
Buber was always punctual, and he used the time before all the other members arrived to clarify technical
matters. He immersed himself in reality.

Q. How was the atmosphere at your meetings with
Buber?

A. Friendly. But after the League stopped meeting, and
I stopped engaging in political activities in 1950, we
did not meet again until my trial. In 1961 I was arrested for meeting with Soviet agents while doing re-

search on my book on Jewish-Arab relations. Buber was a witness at my trial.

Q. What happened?

A. He was very old, but he came to the courthouse and stood in the witness stand for three hours. The prosecutor was a young man who seemed to have never heard of Martin Buber. He asked Buber: "Are you a specialist in Mideastern Studies?" Buber answered: "I am a social anthropologist." The prosecutor pressed: "Then how can you testify about Cohen's work? He is a specialist in Mideastern Studies." Buber answered: "I can sense whether a person is a credible scientist or not." Buber went on to say that if Aharon Cohen is guilty, then Martin Buber is also guilty. He pointed out that the entire trial was absurd, since the topics I had inquired into were topics that he had discussed together with me and with the former president of Israel, Chaim Weitzman. Buber's testimony at my trial can be a lesson in humanity. It was Buber as his true self.

Q. Did you see Buber after you were convicted?

A. Once, while I was serving my sentence, Buber asked the Security Service to allow me to visit him at his home. Buber was ill and could not make the long journey to the north of Israel to visit me, and I wished to consult with him about the book that I was writing. The Security Service agreed and I was transferred to Jerusalem. A young officer took me to Buber's home and listened to the entire discussion between Buber and myself. As we were driving back, he told me that he would never forget this meeting. We discussed Buber's comments on my book, so the discussion was rather technical, but the young officer was very impressed. As Buber was accompanying me to the gate he whispered to me that I should make sure one copy of the book was not in the hands of the Security Service. I told him that I had already sent one copy abroad.

Q. During this meeting did you have an opportunity to discuss your personal situation?

A. No, but Buber did tell me to be very careful, since some of my so-called friends might continue to betray me. In this he was right, since my kibbutz movement's press at first raised objections to having my book published, even though Buber wrote a preface.

Q. Did Buber do anything else to help you during your period of incarceration?

A. He wrote to President Yitschak Ben Zvi, and asked him to pardon me. But Ben Gurion was against it. He was Prime Minister and in charge of the Secret Service, and nobody dared cross his word. The Minister of Justice, Dov Yosef, declared that letting me go free would be a slap to the Secret Service. The Supreme Court declared that the law under which I had been condemned was untenable, and the Knesset changed the law. But that was later. I was released the day after Ben Gurion resigned from being prime minister. On the morrow they released me.—Oh, yes, after Ben Zvi died, Zalman Shazar was nominated for president. He consulted with Buber, and Buber encouraged him to accept the nomination. He added that there was already one good deed waiting to be done: To release Aharon Cohen from jail.

Interview with Avraham Aderet

*(A member of Kibbutz Ayelet Hashachar and
a key educator of the kibbutz movement)*

Q. When did you get to know Buber?

A. In 1963 I met with him quite a bit. I had met with him before that, but not on a regular basis, so I did in 1963.

Q. What were the circumstances that led to these 1963 meetings?

A. Together with other kibbutz members, I was on a committee that was initiating new educational programs for Israeli youth movements that were linked to the kibbutz movement. In these programs there was emphasis on the problems of Israel as a state. Later we wanted to include discussions of the problems of living as a responsible person. We asked Buber to meet with us to formulate this part of our program. The first meeting was very interesting. Then an incident occurred. We planned a meeting on the question: What is life? We hoped that by discussing this question, people could develop criteria for relating to death. We informed Buber of the topic of discussion and invited people to participate. But after I opened and described the topic of discussion, Buber intervened and decided: One cannot discuss such topics and it is forbidden to bring them up, since these are not questions of developing a *Weltanschauung*.

Q. How many people participated in these meetings with Buber?

A. Between eight and twelve.

Q. What kind of atmosphere developed at these meetings?

A. We wanted Buber to guide the meetings. At first he

was enthused by the idea and said: That is the way. But a person sitting in our group could not develop a spiritual relation to Buber. There was a hidden method to the way Buber presented himself. I felt that I was open-minded. But Buber had become accustomed to being an authority, a spiritual authority. He was prepared to speak only with people who accepted his views.

Q. Were these the only meetings you had with Buber?

A. No, I also had personal meetings, not only group meetings when we sat in a circle in his room. The meetings were supposed to be conversations, but both types of meetings ended up being lengthy monologues by Buber.

Q. Were personal topics ever brought up?

A. At times Buber asked a personal question. He might ask a woman if she was married, and had children. I appreciated that. Once I started to relate an incident that happened at my kibbutz and was connected to the topic of discussion. I met with an unwillingness on his part to respond to the topic. He channeled the discussions to the pure theoretical realm.

Q. Why do you think Buber acted this way?

A. I think it had to do with his admiration of the Hasidic way of life that he expressed in many of his writings. He admired the relations between the rabbi and his pupils and emulated them. He was the rabbi. That is also probably one of the reasons that Buber was idolized in Israel, and did not find a way to link himself to any specific group. My impression is that his philosophy of dialogue found little expression in his daily life. He liked to hear himself. When I sat with him I did not feel that he listened to me. He related to me as an It. Once at a group meeting we were discussing

"Love your neighbor as yourself." I tried to bring up an opposing view to what he had expressed. He did not want to listen.

Q. Do you believe that Buber felt his isolation?

A. I don't believe that Buber viewed his being isolated as a tragedy. He seemed unable to relate to the man in the street, and did not seem to appreciate the realm of action. I felt something cold in his personality.

Q. Was there any development in your relations with Buber?

A. In the first meetings his face was interesting and there was light in his eyes, and I felt something spiritual. Later my impression changed. For instance, I often felt that there was something non-Jewish about him. The language he spoke, the style of his speaking. It seemed sterile. As if from another world, not the world that we shared together. And as I said, he was not open-minded.

Q. Were his answers to your questions clear?

A. Very clear. He had a unique style, and at times played with the language. But in these clear answers I often felt a lack of modesty, or perhaps that is my impression because he liked so much to play with language and with the style of his responses. And perhaps this lack of modesty and over-styling did not allow him to convey the spirit of what he was saying.

Interview with A. Elhanani

(Journalist for the Israeli Newspaper
Davar *in Jerusalem)*

Q. How did you get to know Buber?

A. I was a journalist for the Israeli newspaper *Davar* in Jerusalem for many years, and I would meet quite regularly with writers and intellectuals. I believe that it was S.Y. Agnon who suggested to Buber that he call on me, and Buber did.

Q. What did he call on you for?

A. At times newspapers would publish reports about Buber that were not true, or were farfetched. Then he would usually call me up and ask what to do. I would usually respond by saying: "Let's first get the facts straight—then you can publish a denial." At first, I was a bit apprehensive about going to meet him—after all, he was very famous—but during the meetings I felt very comfortable. We would meet in his study, which was full of books with a lamp above Buber's table. And Buber gave me the feeling that I was talking person to person with someone who was really concerned with the fate of our world. Later I wrote a few articles about him in my newspaper in which I tried to popularize his thinking for our readers.

Q. What do you mean when you say you felt that Buber was concerned with the fate of the world?

A. Well, you felt as if he knew what needed to be done. For instance, he once told me that after the Soviet Union had exploded its megaton nuclear bomb, a rich man in Switzerland asked Buber to organize a meeting of intellectuals from around the world, including the Soviet Union, to respond to this development. That person was willing to pay all the expenses for such a meeting. Buber set only one condition. He demanded that it be kept secret. It didn't work out, though.

Q. Why did Buber want it to be kept secret?

A. So that people could speak their mind freely, so that they wouldn't be afraid to speak their mind.

Q. What were your impressions from your meetings with Buber?

A. One lasting impression was that Buber had no indigenous student—in other words, no Israelis would define themselves as students of Martin Buber. Those who defined themselves as followers of Martin Buber were all Jews from Germany. I felt that, perhaps for this reason, he was very lonely in Israel.

Q. Did you feel free to come to Buber's house, or were all your visits with some goal in mind?

A. I always came with some goal in mind. You see, Buber did not mix with Israeli society. He rarely left his house to come to a public place, like a movie, or a theatre or a concert. He would laugh with all his heart at times, but I never heard him tell a joke, and I met him many times over the years. Perhaps one point worth adding is that in Buber's study he always used a lamp. It was always dark with artificial lighting. He never opened the blinds and let the full light of day stream in.

Interview with Samuel Eisenstadt

*(Professor of Sociology at Hebrew University
One of Buber's first doctoral students)*

Q. When did you get to know Buber?

A. I studied for my MA under his guidance in the years 1940 to 1944, and for my Ph.D. under his guidance from 1944 to 1947.

Q. In what area?

A. Sociology of civilization.

Q. What kind of atmosphere prevailed in Buber's classes?

A. Informal, open. He taught in a well-organized manner, he encouraged discussion. In his seminars discussion and dialogue were most important.

Q. How many students participated in his classes?

A. In the lectures, between forty and forty-five and in the seminars, around twenty.

Q. Was there ever an atmosphere of genuine dialogue in the classroom, I mean where people felt free to bring up personal problems?

A. No, personal problems were not brought up, only problems that had to do with the material being studied.

Q. Did Buber interact with students during the break?

A. One could approach him. In general, Buber was open when someone approached him. Later I approached him asking his support in getting a job. Personally, I had many meetings with him.

Q. Did he lecture clearly and make sure that he was understood?

A. Very clearly.

Q. Did you ever feel that Buber did something wrong?

A. I believe that at times he had too much patience, and allowed people to take up class time with foolish questions.

Q. Did he only teach, or was he also concerned with the education of his pupils' character?

A. He did not formally educate our character. But he had an image that educated, and whoever was impressed by it was educated.

Q. Did he ever speak to you or to others about the realization of his educational philosophy?

A. In personal discussions. During the first year he met with me quite a bit and lent me books to read that had to do with the topic of the lecture, or about sociology and anthropology, and we would meet and discuss what I had read.

Q. What was Buber's role as your mentor in guiding you to write an MA and a doctoral dissertation?

A. He lent me books, we discussed the topic of my study, but in general he let me go my own way.

Q. Why did you choose to do your Ph.D. under Buber?

A. It was natural, since he was the only person at the university who could be a director for a dissertation in sociology.

Q. Did you meet regularly?

A. Whenever I needed to, I'd call Buber up and set up a meeting.

Q. What did you learn from Buber as a mentor?

A. I was impressed by the broadness of his knowledge. He knew sociology from a world perspective. He did not confine his sociological thought to one country or milieu. He was like a grandfather to me. I think that the great difference in our ages—forty-five years— made our relations easier. He kept a natural distance because of this age difference, and I felt nothing uncomfortable.

Q. After you finished your Ph.D. did you continue to keep up relations with Buber?

A. Yes, and we had excellent relations. He was later my boss in the sociology department, and now I am his heir. Whenever I returned from abroad I'd come to see him. He was interested in me and helped me in my academic career. I know that he was an actor, but with me he acted the role of the "Good Grandfather."

Interview with Joseph Ben Dov

(Professor at Hebrew University)

Q. I understand that you took some classes that Buber taught?

A. Yes, in 1944 to 1946 I took some of his classes in sociology of civilization at the Hebrew University.

Q. Could you describe the atmosphere in class?

A. It was pleasant. Buber would always start off by asking us to summarize what had been discussed at the previous meeting, perhaps because he didn't remember where he had stopped. In the seminars it was also pleasant. I was impressed by Buber as a person, by his politeness, and his attempting to relate personally to his students. He did not participate much in the seminar. We read Marx and were not impressed by Buber's scientific interpretation. He related to the text mainly in the manner of: With this part I agree, and with this view I disagree. Still, he encouraged us to work. He created an atmosphere of personal relations and of an intellectual and aesthetic experience. He always tried to find the precise word for what he was trying to convey. But with all this, I must admit that I did not learn much sociology from Buber.

Q. How many students participated in his lectures?

A. From ten to around twenty-seven.

Q. What was his method of teaching?

A. Regular lecturing, and in the seminars he taught like other teachers. He gave you, though, the impression of presence. He was less an intellectual than other teachers and more of an educator.

Q. Did you ever speak of personal problems in class?

A. At times Buber would mention personal encounters, like an argument he once had with Max Weber. It seemed that Weber did not appreciate what Buber was doing and Buber viewed him as an opponent. In general, Buber did not bring up personal problems.

Q. Did you meet with Buber outside the class?

A. Buber always met with pupils at his home, which was what most teachers did at that time. His attitude toward students was good, but he kept his distance. Worse, Buber had very little sensitivity to the fact that he was very affluent while most of his students were poor. He would sit behind his desk and every so often take a piece of chocolate from his drawer and pop it into his mouth without ever offering a piece to the student, who being poor, could not afford to spend money on chocolate. So, in addition to being impolite, he was insensitive. We had a feeling that he was behaving like a Polish nobleman.

Q. Did he ask you about personal problems?

A. If he did—less than other teachers.

Q. Were his lectures clear?

A. Pretty clear. He tried to explain himself.

Q. What were your impressions of Buber as a lecturer?

A. One did not get the impression that Buber was a sociologist in the technical sense of the term. He used sociological writings in order to express himself. In his seminars, though, he did encourage us to think independently and to express ourselves. But Buber was generally more interested in sharing his own intellectual experiences with us than in conveying knowledge. Here I must add that he was a superb actor. He acted himself very well, and his act was very impressive. He conveyed the feeling that here is a very wise man who knows many languages, and whose knowledge is impressive. His personality was an aesthetic creation, like a great statue.

Q. In summary, what are your lasting feelings about Buber?

A. Very ambivalent. Meeting with him was an aesthetic experience. I admired his manner of behavior, his ability to express himself. But still, despite my being close to his political views, to his propounding Jewish-Arab understanding, I always felt that I had something against Buber. I think this resentment was a result of two of Buber's attitudes, not of his views. First, I resented his acting as if he were part of the nobility, an attitude that emerged despite his attempts to be personal with his students. He definitely viewed himself as being somewhat above us. Second, I was angry at him for being a Jew for the Gentiles, and on the other hand not being a Jew among Jews. I resented him calling Jesus his "elder brother." He seemed to relate to Judaism as someone who is above or beyond it, not as someone who is part of it. Hence I saw it as grotesque when some Jews saw him as their spiritual leader. I viewed him more as a traitor.

Interview with Benno Frank

(Theatre Director and Director of plays)

Q. When did you first meet Buber?

A. I grew up in Frankfurt in a period of nihilism after the First World War. I was educated to be an orthodox Jew; but after a while I began rebelling against the precepts of orthodox Jewry. My relations with my father were always icy, and when I rebelled against orthodox Jewry I suddenly felt alone, very alone. I began frequenting the lectures given at the Jewish Lehrhaus, and participating in the dramatic club there. Because of my inner conflicts I also started considering suicide. Life seemed meaningless to me. Suddenly I had no vocation, and after abandoning the yeshiva in which I had studied, I did not know how to go about acquiring a vocation. I once spoke about my situation to Franz Rosenzweig, who was in charge of the Lehrhaus, even though he was already ill. I believe that he alerted Buber to my situation, because, after I had participated in a Purim play, where Buber was in the audience, he chose an opportunity after his next lecture and took me aside and helped me unburden myself. I told him how I felt. And then he said a sentence that became a direction for my life: "Become an actor: On the stage you will be able to live many lives and to die many deaths." That is exactly what I did. I became an actor and a director.

Q. Did you continue to meet with Buber?

A. Not frequently. But our paths crossed again and again, and I kept up contact because I was indebted to him. I met him a few times when he came to Israel and I was teaching drama at the Hebrew University and was a director of a theatre. Later I invited him to my home

94

when he visited the States and I was living there for a while.

Q. What characterized the meetings?

A. Well, you have to understand what meeting with Buber was all about. Buber was open-minded and willing to listen. He related to you personally. Still, a dialogue with him was a sort of climbing to an intellectual peak; it was not a discussion about everyday things. Buber was, in my view, obsessed with two things: work and the word. He never responded casually, and when I met with him I never had the feeling that it could be a casual meeting, for the fun of it. And his obsession with words resembled, at least in my eyes, a sexual obsession. He loved words and was always seeking for the correct exact word. Often he found it. I believe that because of these two obsessions he had few friends. It is hard to develop friendships when one is fascinated by words.

Q. What else impressed you in your meetings with Buber?

*A.*Since I was not very interested in philosophy, it was the little things that impressed me. I remember that in Germany Paula Buber wore a cross around her neck. When she emigrated to Israel she removed it. I remember Buber's enormous library and his ability to find any book he sought. I was always impressed by how lonely Buber must be. In Germany he was a Jew. When he reached Israel, he did not become an Israeli—in many respects he remained a German. For instance, he wrote his books in German. I remember Buber's not mixing with other people, and that after a meeting with him I would go home with the feeling that it was difficult to digest him.

Q. In addition to that first significant meeting, did Buber influence you personally?

A. Of course. His entire image and views influenced me deeply, but it is difficult for me to articulate how and where. I do remember that he once answered me beautifully when I asked him; "When should I tell a person something straightforwardly?" Buber replied; "You can be straightforward in many instances. If you tell a person something that is either true, or necessary, or kind, you are in the right direction. But if it is two of the above three then you can rest assured that it is good to be straightforward. Thus if something is true and necessary or true and kind, it is good to say it. But if something is not necessary and is unkind, I would refrain from saying it, even if it were true. I would also not say something that is kind if it were neither necessary nor true." I have followed this rule since then and have found it to be very good.

Q. What were your impressions of the relations between Buber and Paula?

A. Because he was obsessed with work, Buber needed a woman in the house to take care of his everyday needs. Paula fit this role very well. You must understand that Buber was in many ways a remnant of the Jewish aristocracy. He always acted formally toward you, and that, of course, influenced the sort of relations that he built with Paula. I believe that these relations were behind his saying; "it is very difficult to educate one's children, less difficult with one's grandchildren, and rather simple with one's great-grandchildren." In any event, I believe that it was Paula who helped Buber make his home into his castle.

First Interview with
Menachem (Hermann) Gerson

(Close to Buber in Germany; established youth movement
Werkleute *under Buber's influence.*
He later became a member of Kibbutz Hazorea.)

Q. Describe your first meeting with Buber.

A. I come from a family of assimilated Jews, very assimilated. Only around the age of eighteen did I reach
the decision that I wanted to be a Jew. Now it looks
natural, but when I mentioned this decision in the
youth movement to which I belonged, people thought
I was insane. It was during this period that I encountered Buber's writings, specifically his essays on Judaism, and I felt that they were of great assistance to
me in my situation. The situation of wanting to renew my relations to Judaism. I read these essays in
1926, my first year of studies at Berlin University.
Later I also studied at the Jewish Hochschule. In the
same year, Buber came to give a lecture in Berlin,
which I attended. I don't remember the topic he discussed, but he deeply impressed me. It was like light-
ning. I suddenly knew that Buber was the person I
had been seeking to guide me.

Q. What did you do?

A. I wrote Buber a letter and asked him to be my spiritual mentor. Buber had made it a custom to answer
every letter that he received. I have adopted this custom also. It was, of course, not an ordinary event that
a young person approached him with such a request.
He responded, and a short time later he reached Berlin, in November 1926, and invited me to his hotel.
We sat and drank coffee, and my first impression of

97

Buber was that I never before saw a person put so much sugar in a small cup of coffee, seven teaspoons of sugar. A discussion developed, and from then on we would meet whenever Buber came to Berlin. I also visited him a few times a year in Heppenheim. In addition I wrote him many letters. He could not always answer all my questions, but he answered many of them. It was a strong and continuous communication. Later I learned that in many respects I was somewhat of an envoy for Buber; I conveyed to him much of what was happening in Berlin.

Q. I understand that under Buber's influence you established a Jewish youth movement called *Werkleute*?

A. Yes. We followed Buber in the idea that before one returns to Zionism one must return to Judaism. It was a movement for assimilated Jewish youth. In other words, we did not stress going to Israel. Before that we wanted to live our Judaism. That demanded not only political Zionism as Herzl envisioned it, but also a return to reading the sources of Judaism. This return to the sources in order to live differently is, I believe, one of Buber's important contributions to Judaism.

Q. Can you describe in detail what you did?

A. Buber knew that the young people to whom he was speaking did not know Hebrew. That is probably the reason he decided, together with Franz Rosenzweig, to translate the Bible—so that assimilated Jewish youths could read a text that would be very faithful to the Hebrew source. What characterized the *Werkleute* was that at first we did not think of going to Israel. We stressed that as members of the Jewish nation we must return to Jewish sources. Our plan was to remain in Germany where we felt at home. Furthermore, under Buber's influence, who was a major influence on our movement through me, we believed that one can serve God and Judaism everywhere. We believed that the large city was the destiny of contemporary man, and since there is no place where God is not present, we planned to stay in a large city and to fulfill what Buber called a true commune.

Q. What did you do?

A. A true commune, according to Buber, has two characteristics. First, it is linked to one value center. Second, the relations between the persons in the commune are direct and informal. We wanted to live and to work as Jews, but we were also socialists. We wanted to join a small party in Germany that was ideologically situated between the socialists and the communists. We also wanted our relations to be direct and informal. But that was not realistic. We established a school for Jewish youth in Berlin, in which we tried to realize what we had learned from Buber about the necessity of returning to Judaism. Once the Nazis arrested me for my work in that school. We also tried to organize Jewish cultural events in other cities in Germany.

Q. Was Buber linked to the school that you established? Did he visit it?

A. He knew about the school through me.

Q. Didn't he meet with other members of the *Werkleute?*

A. He met with them much later. He came to us only once, at one of our congresses. Later Eliezer Beeri from our movement also got to know Buber through Buber's granddaughters. We changed our direction when Hitler came to power on January 30, 1933. In February of that year we started organizing a *Hachshara*, a training farm so that we could learn agriculture in order to go to Israel. Buber agreed that this was the right thing to do. We knew that in Israel we could try to realize Buber's beliefs much more easily than in a Germany headed by Hitler. At that time Buber took upon himself to establish an institution for teaching German Jews about their Judaism. It was very important for the assimilated Jews who were being persecuted as Jews. They felt that they were linked to Judaism without knowing what Judaism was all about. Buber wanted to help them return to Judaism. He asked me to serve as his secretary in this endeavor, but I refused.

Q. When did you last see Buber in Germany?

A. I don't remember the last visit or how we parted. I left Germany in 1934. But I do remember that one of my last visits was a day after the Nazis searched Buber's house in Heppenheim and Paula got enraged and screamed at them. When I arrived from Berlin they arrested me and accused me of being Buber's secret link to subversive activities in Berlin. They let me out after I spent twenty-four hours in prison. I also remember that Buber wanted to come to the Hebrew University in Jerusalem, but they did not want to accept him as a specialist in the field of religion. It's a terrible story. Now the Hebrew University views him as one of its heroes, but they didn't want him as a religious philosopher. He told me all about it many years later, after he had already retired, when I met him in Switzerland on one of the hills above Lucerne. But around the time that Buber reached Israel our relations broke down—for twenty years.

Q. In one of your articles on Buber, you wrote that your relations with him broke down more because of your

adherence to Freud than because of your adherence to
Marx. Can you clarify this point?

A. There is a personal and a general aspect to my answer.
When I went through a frustrating period with my
first wife, I wrote to Buber that I had decided to
undergo psychoanalytic treatment. He was very unhappy with my decision, and reminded me of the
German legend where a person took out someone's
living heart and replaced it with a heart of stone. He
held that such would happen to me in the treatment.
I did undergo the treatment. But Buber's response
cooled our relations until they broke off. And since I
was the person who linked our group to Buber, his
relations with the group also broke down. But there
is a more general aspect to the breakdown of our relations with Buber. He taught us about a commune,
but he taught it in too idyllic a manner, and we could
not live what he taught. He did not prepare us for the
difficulties that we would encounter in our everyday
life. He did not relate to a fact prominent in Freud's
thinking, that people also have desires. I told him all
this in a private conversation when I came to celebrate
his eighty-fifth birthday. Buber's answer was: "At that
time I did not know." I admired him for this answer
and for his ability to admit to a man thirty years his
junior how he had failed him. But to get back to the
breakdown in relations, Buber was not happy that we
joined the Hashomer Hatzair kibbutz movement. I
think that added to the entire situation.

Q. Was Buber far removed from your political views? Is
that why he was against your joining the Hashomer
Hatzair kibbutz movement?

A. No, he wasn't. He once told Hazan and myself that

he had always voted for Mapam, our political party, because of its stance on the Arab question. But he also told us that he did not agree with some of our ideas, and therefore he could not become a party member. But he voted for us and against Ben Gurion, whom he saw as a political adversary, at least in terms of values. He was angry that Ben Gurion had diminished the significance of the *Halutz*, the pioneer. And he was angry at the way Ben Gurion dealt with the Arabs.

Q. Were you influenced by Buber's educational thought?

A. Not really. I don't think that there is a possibility of dialogue in education or that a teacher can attempt to base his manner of relating to students on Buber's dialogical philosophy.

Q. Did you have any relations with other members of Buber's family?

A. Formal relations, since I visited them. I believe that his wife was a dominating person with much influence on his life. She left her religion and her family when she came to live with him. She told me once: "I know what it means to close a door and to never open it again." She was a strong and very talented woman. She told me once that she could never leave the children in Buber's charge, and added jokingly, he would simply close them in a drawer of his desk and forget about them. So she guarded him from his children, but in another sense she helped him not become a remote intellectual. She often connected him to reality.

Second Interview
with Menachem (Hermann) Gerson

Q. How did Buber influence life in Kibbutz Hazorea—
if at all?

A. Buber once asked me that question when I visited him
in Jerusalem after our relations had been renewed. I
answered, "Consideration for the individual." We
learned from Buber that the kibbutz must be consid-
erate toward its individual members. I believe that we
are conveying this important message to the coming
generation. Unlike other kibbutzim, we strive to leave
a private realm around each individual where kibbutz
interest and gossip don't enter. We allow the individual room to live.

Q. Could you add a bit to what you said previously concerning Buber's relationship to Freud and psychoanalysis?

A. I already mentioned that Buber was against my going
to an analyst when I underwent a frustrating period
with my first wife. I do not think that I mentioned
that Buber married me to my first wife. In Germany
at that period, any person could conduct a marriage,
and Buber married me to my first wife. When I decided to go to analysis, he notified me that he would
never again take upon himself the responsibility to
marry a couple—that my marriage would be the first
and last time he did something like this. He also added
that he would write a strong article against Freud, but
as far as I know Buber never wrote the article. By the
way, he did send me a supportive letter when I was
divorced. I think that, essentially, Buber believed in
the whole person and was against the dissecting ten-

dency in Freud's work. He thought that Freud did not see the entire person.

Q. When your relations with Buber were renewed, was he interested in what was happening in Kibbutz Hazorea?

A. The renewed relationship was only with Eliezer Beeri and myself. Buber did not visit the kibbutz. You see, his connection to the *Werkleute* was only through me, which was a mistake I made back in Germany—I was young. When the relationship was renewed, it was renewed only with those who previously had had a relationship with him. I remember that I once told Buber that the younger generation of Kibbutz members are living in the kibbutz not because of ideology, but because they feel at home in the kibbutz. He replied that such an attitude is inhuman.

Q. When you visited Buber, did you take your wife along?

A. No, she came only once.

Q. Can you point out an important area where Buber helped you?

A. I believe that his most important help came when I was establishing the *Werkleute*. My theory was that the ideals of the youth movement need not vanish when the period of youth fades, and that one can continue to attempt to realize those ideals throughout one's entire life. In this original approach Buber supported me wholeheartedly, even though he did not always answer the questions or provide solutions to the many problems that I posed.

Q. Did Buber ever meet with Arabs?

A. No, I don't think that he did except in formal meetings. I doubt that he ever met with an Arab for a conversation, the way he conversed with Jews and

Christians. But he always held that one must meet with the Arabs.

Q. Did you always feel comfortable visiting Buber?

A. I did. But I know that other people felt otherwise. Yonina Talmon, who wrote her Ph.D. dissertation under Buber, was very vehement about how insensitive Buber and Paula were. At times she would come to him for a morning meeting after spending the entire night on guard duty at the Hebrew University. During the meeting Paula would enter and bring Buber coffee and cake, and neither of them would offer Yonina anything. And this happened more than once, and they knew that she had been on guard duty. I did not encounter such insensitivity, perhaps because we had already established relations in Germany. Perhaps Buber's being used to living affluently made him insensitive to the situation of his students. Yonina added criticisms of Buber as a teacher—that he often assumed the pose of a prophet, and then one could not learn anything from him.

Q. What is your major criticism of Buber as a person?

A. I would say that in certain significant areas he did not have the courage of his convictions. Here was a man who worked for Zionism, wrote about Zionism, and taught about Zionism, who did not reach Israel until the age of sixty—after Hitler came to power and threatened his very existence in Germany, and only after being offered a chair at the Hebrew University. The same is true about his relationship to utopian socialism. He wrote about utopian socialism, but he never tried to live it. A second criticism is that he often lapsed into the pose of a prophet. I remember that he once was invited to Oranim, a kibbutz teacher-training institute. I met with the students before his visit and suggested that they ask Buber questions that really concerned them, otherwise he would assume the pose of a prophet. This was in the late fifties or early sixties. Well, they asked general questions, and as I had predicted, Buber assumed the pose of a prophet in answering them. Only when Buber felt that you were turning to him with something significant in your life did he stop being an actor.

Interview with Gustav Horn

(Member of Werkleute and later of Kibbutz Hazorea)

Q. When did you first meet Buber?

A. In 1929 in Cologne. We (the *Werkleute*) had set up a house for Jewish youth in that city, and for the dedication Buber was invited to give a speech. When I approached him after his speech I was already under his influence. I was impressed by the straightforwardness of his conversation and by his attentiveness to each person. After the speech he gave a Bible lesson and convinced us to read and understand the Bible. But in the *Werkleute* we were influenced by Buber primarily through Menachem Gerson.

Q. Did you ever meet personally with Buber in those years?

A. In 1932 and 1933 I met with him a few times. I was thinking of writing a doctoral dissertation on Max Scheler and I consulted with Buber. He also helped us raise funds to buy land for the *Werkleute*.

Q. Did Buber help in fundraising?

A. Not directly. He wrote to Rupin and to Weitzman about acquiring land for us in Israel. He also wrote to rich Jews in Germany who could contribute to the fund for buying land. I met with him again in 1934 in connection with the upcoming convention of the Hechalutz movement, where Buber was invited to give a speech on the *Weltanschauung* of the Chalutz. We met a few times beforehand to discuss that speech. Afterward I did not renew contact with Buber until 1958.

Q. After the convention you didn't see Buber again until 1958?

A. No, in 1935 Buber gave some Bible lessons at Hechalutz meetings. I saw him there. But after we came to Israel there was a long break in relations.

Q. How were you influenced by Buber?

A. I was more influenced by his understanding of the commune than by his views on Judaism. I had a feeling that his views on Judaism were for youths who were partly assimilated. His writings helped them accept Judaism. I came from a nonassimilated liberal Jewish home, and his writings on Judaism did not speak to me as they spoke to others. Often I argued against these views. In the *Werkleute* we were greatly influenced by Buber's writings on the commune, which, as adults, we wanted to realize. At first we wanted to set up a commune in Germany that would be a continuation of our life in the youth movement. Later, after Hitler came to power, we decided to set up a commune in Israel.

Q. Did you feel that you realized Buber's commune in the kibbutz?

A. That was our dream, but reality was different. I believe that the kibbutz does try to bring people to be straightforward with each other.

Q. Why was there such a long period in which you had no contact with Buber?

A. Buber influenced us during the early 1930s. He then remained in Hitler's Germany to teach Jews to struggle against Nazism by learning Jewish sources. We left Hitler and Germany behind and went to the kibbutz; when Buber came to Israel in 1938 he didn't contact his former pupils or groups close to us. Instead he attached himself to the Hebrew University and lived in a sort of ivory tower. That led to our separation from him.

Q. Do you remember any interesting incidents from your meetings with Buber?

A. I remember his courage. At the Hechalutz convention that I mentioned he attacked the Jewish revisionists. But he did it in a philosophical manner, while hinting that he was also attacking the Nazis. There was a clerk from the Gestapo at the meeting. He sent a note to the chairman saying that Buber's speech was political and against the law. The chairman sent a note back saying that Buber was only talking philosophy, and the Gestapo clerk let it pass. But we all knew that the speech had political implications.

Q. How did Buber relate to you when you visited him?

A. Cordially. We were very impressed by the fact that such an important person was willing to meet with each of us and to discuss the problems that we brought up. It was pleasant to meet with him. He saw you as a unique person.

Interview with Zvi Werblovski

(Professor of Religion at Hebrew University)

Q. When did you first meet Buber?

A. Even as a youth I heard about Buber and his thought, but I did not meet him until 1956, when I arrived in Israel to join the department of religious sciences at the Hebrew University. I was therefore close to Buber's area of interest, even though he had already retired. In that year we set up the Interfaith Commission of Israel, and I met with Buber to invite him to be our first honorary president.

Q. What do you remember from this first meeting?

A. I remember his large desk and many books. One of my lasting memories was that when I would meet with Buber at his home, even for a period of two or three hours, he would never offer me anything to drink. There was something lacking in his sensitivity toward other people. I never had an experience of genuine dialogue in my meetings with him, even though many people whom I value and respect did describe such an experience. It didn't happen to me.

Q. How did you feel at your meetings with Buber?

A. I loathe the hero-worship that was part of the atmosphere encompassing Buber. When I met with him, I found it difficult to distinguish between what was authentic and what was an act. My feeling was that he consistently played the role of the great prophet; when I asked a question he would adopt a demeanor of deep thought, and would answer only after a few minutes, as if after profound consideration. I didn't believe in this act; I thought the answer was ready beforehand. In short, since I'm a cold-thinking pragmatic person,

Buber's playing the prophet made me feel very uncomfortable.

Q. Can you tell about other incidents in which you met with Buber?

A. After the Eichmann trial a group of us got together and wrote to the president against having Eichmann hanged. Buber hosted the meeting and he received all the attention of the press in this matter, but he was one among many. It was an exciting meeting, though, because there were many people there at Buber's house who were very critical of Buber, but who joined him and us in being against capital punishment for Eichmann.

Q. Did Buber know that you were critical of him?

A. He knew that I was not among his followers.

Q. What was his response?

A. Dignified and correct. He did not hold it against me when I needed his help. Once I needed a book that he had that could not be found anywhere else in Jerusalem, and he willingly lent me the book. People were surprised at his willingness. You see, many people associated me with the group around Gershom Scholem, who criticized Buber. But I think that this division into groups is superficial, because Buber is at a totally different level than Scholem.

Q. Do you recall any other areas in which your path crossed with Buber's?

A. I met with him about making changes in the program of the Ministry of Education concerning Arabs, and Buber encouraged me in this work. That was part of my work as president of the Israel Interfaith Commission.

Q. Were you critical of Buber's writings?

A. One of my main criticisms is that Buber had no relation to Halachah, while I believe that Halachah is central to Judaism and has been so for hundreds of years. Jewish consciousness flows in the channel of Halachah, and Buber had no relationship to this flow. I tell my students that, for this reason, Buber's relationship to Judaism was similar to a person who had no relationship to sex.

Interview with Michael Wyschogrod

(Professor of Philosophy at CUNY)

Q. When did you first meet Buber?

A. I think that it was in 1953 when Buber came to the United States and lectured at the Jewish Theological Seminary. The Seminary organized a dinner in his honor; I believe it was one day after he arrived. At the dinner, he spoke with great clarity. After dinner, there were some people around him, and I went up and introduced myself and asked if I could meet with him privately. Buber opened his pocket calendar, and I remember that he had one of those old fountain pens that you opened and closed by screwing the cover on, and he asked me when it would be convenient for me to come. We set up a meeting, and during the period that he was in New York we met quite often. I also participated in a learning group at the Seminary that he held every Saturday afternoon, in which various questions were brought up and discussed. It was not a lecture, but a free discussion period with Buber. I remember that I had to sleep at the Seminary in order to participate in these meetings, since I don't ride on the Sabbath, but I did it for many weeks because I wanted to participate in those meetings.

Q. Do you remember any significant incident during those meetings?

A. I remember one significant incident that occurred shortly after Buber arrived in New York. On the first Friday evening, the Jewish Theological Seminary organized a Sabbath meal in his honor. After the meal, Buber was supposed to get to his hotel, which was about fifty blocks from where we were. It was ten o'clock at night, and a cold rain was falling. None of us would ride or drive on the Sabbath, and we did not know how Buber would get to his hotel. We knew that he didn't mind riding on the Sabbath and asked him if we should hail him a cab. We were quite unhappy to do this, because we are not supposed to encourage another Jew to ride on the Sabbath, but since Buber was an elderly man and the weather was bad, we felt that it was all right. But Buber answered, "No, I'll walk." And so all of us decided to accompany him. We all walked along Broadway with him for fifty blocks and arrived at the hotel wet. He was wet also, but he had felt that it was not appropriate to ride in a cab.

Q. Did you feel that Buber personally realized his thought?

A. Some people are better in their books than in their lives, and I've met such people. But I felt that Buber, the person, was often greater than his books. When he sat with you he gave you his full attention. Only you existed. This ability to listen and to give you the feeling that he was waiting for you, as you are, influenced people. When he lectured, he was best at creating a dialogue or a conversation with anyone who asked him a question. Buber was also open to listening to anyone who approached him. In short, he was a gentleman, he was cordial, he was sensitive, and he was willing to listen and to respond on the deepest level that the question required.

Interview with Aliza Ziv Or

(Teacher living in Jerusalem.
She was a student of Buber.)

Q. When did you first meet Buber?

A. I came from an assimilated family in Munich, and I got to know Buber through his writings before I met him. Since I was born in 1915, I reached the age of 18 when Hitler came to power. We Jews needed someone to help us respond to antisemitism, and I found that Buber's writings helped me, much more than the writings of Herzl or Pinsker. One might say that he helped us to straighten our back. I first met Buber when I took some of his classes at the Hebrew University a few years later. We were about ten students in his class on sociology of religion. We got to know each other, but I did not become close to Buber, perhaps because at that time my main area of interest was Oriental Studies. During the period that I took his class, I would walk home with Buber, since we were both going in the same direction. After that year I did not meet him again until in 1952, when I took some courses at the Seminar for National Teachers that Buber helped establish.

Q. How did you feel when you and Buber walked home together?

A. I felt as if there was a barrier that divided us and that Buber made great attempts to break that barrier, but did not succeed. Students admired the wealth of his knowledge, but they did not feel close to him. I really don't know why, because we did feel close to other teachers like Scholem, Bergmann, or Nechama Lebovitz. Perhaps it was because we felt uncomfortable with how Buber expressed his Judaism. But it was also his style and his personality that aroused us to not accept him, even though we acknowledged the greatness of his work, such as *I and Thou*. This lack of acceptance of Buber continued in my case for many years; I remember that I once even felt uncomfortable having his books in my house, and I gave them all away. Now I read his books with less anger, I seem to forgive him. I also came to his eightieth birthday party.

Q. Can you say a bit more about why you were so opposed to Buber?

A. I only know that I was then very antiromantic in my approach to literature and the arts. I hated the music of Wagner and Mahler, and the writings of Hesse, Kafka, and Rilke, and others whom I thought romantic. I liked the classics, Goethe, for instance. Therefore, I really didn't like Buber's style; there were moments when I loathed it, despised it. I was afraid of all his mysticism; to me it looked counterfeit, and had nothing to do with us or with our life. Now I see things differently. I think that Buber wanted to touch deep levels, and perhaps I wasn't prepared for that. Buber wanted to arouse people, and he didn't reach me.

Q. How were the classes Buber gave at the Seminar?

A. I remember the entire period as very exciting and exhilarating, but Buber's classes, which were well attended because of his fame, were not very successful.

Q. Why not?

A. For instance, Buber started with a discussion of relationships between persons, and he made it into something that we felt was mystical. Participants in the class could not digest what he was teaching. Then Buber turned to one student and said: "I'm sure that this has happened to you." . . . In some way he was trying to reach our hearts, and he failed.

Q. Could you perhaps describe one such class that Buber taught?

A. I clearly remember a class that he taught on Isaiah's vision. Buber presented an approach and the students argued with him. There were many arguments. Buber answered every question, even if it was stupid. He seemed to make a point to honor everyone there, even if someone said stupid things. But all these questionings and honorings led to a situation where the lesson lost all clear sense of direction. Instead of learning something, we were participating in a happening. Today I believe that we were also partially responsible for all this, since Buber wanted, in his manner, to come close to us and to teach us. But we did not allow him, we rejected him. I always remember his classes at the Seminar, not as an intellectual or personally meaningful experience, but rather as a curiosity, a happening.

Q. Did students get excited in his classes?

A. Yes, but it was not the excitement of learning something, it was the excitement of having someone to attack. With other teachers there was excitement about learning. I think that Hugo Bergmann succeeded in realizing Buber's philosophy in his classes. But Buber's classes were undisciplined and chaotic. I find this to be sad, since Buber once told me when I walked home with him, "I'd like young people to work and to think." But he did not know how to encourage such work and thought with us. He was happy when students approached him, but I'm not sure he touched their lives.

Q. Was Buber ever angry, or did he ever express anger?

A. Once I borrowed a book from him and did not return it for a long time. He then wrote me an angry postcard. But at the Seminar he always acted like a gentleman. He did not get angry even when there were political arguments. I must add that there was also something unattractive about Buber's entire appearance. A large beard and behind it a small body. He sometimes reminded me of a cartoon.

Q. Did Buber have a sense of humor?

A. He understood humor, but he had no sense of humor. He was always very very serious, but he did not get angry when someone expressed something funny.

Q. Were you ever at his home?

A. No, I was never that close to him.

Q. How would you summarize your relationship to Buber?

A. I believe that we were rather unfair to him. He wanted to be close to us, and we rejected him because he seemed to touch points that were tender, and we wanted to be strong and tough. To some extent his greatness can perhaps be seen in the strong responses that he aroused. Yes, at times we acted like pigs. We were not honest enough to learn to be against Buber, so we found ways of evading him and his thoughts.

Interview with Yehuda Yeari

(Writer and Editor living in Jerusalem. He helped Buber publish his books in Hebrew.)

Q. When did you first meet Buber?

A. I was born in Galicia. At the age of nineteen, in 1920, I decided to go to Israel to live, together with a group of students. On the way we stopped in Prague to participate in a convention of young Zionists, in which representatives from Israel also participated. Among the featured speakers at the convention were Hugo Bergmann, A.D. Gordon, and Martin Buber. I saw Buber there, but I didn't get to know him until a bit later. After the convention we spent several weeks getting used to hard work and waiting for our visas at a youth village that was administered by a psychoanalyst called Siegfried, who was a friend of Martin Buber. We learned a bit about agricultural work there and also encountered the free education that prevailed in this village. I should perhaps add that in my group all the people were students except me. I had received a traditional education at home, and when I wanted to become a student, the war interfered. I was the only one in the group who had no general education, and I felt very lonely and alienated. At the village we used to take long walks on the Sabbath, and on one of these walks in which Buber participated he called me and asked me to walk alongside him. He put his hand on my shoulder. That gesture deeply impressed me, since Buber was so famous. I wondered why he had chosen me. He asked me about Hasidism and I told him what I knew from my experience. He listened. After that meeting I decided to read his books, even though I did not become one of his adherents.

Q. When did you meet Buber again?

A. When I came to Israel I first joined Kibbutz Beit Alpha, in which some members called themselves students of Buber. After a few years I left the kibbutz
and moved to Jerusalem. I believe it was 1932 when
Buber visited Jerusalem and stayed with Hugo Bergmann. I had become close to Bergmann in Prague.
Bergmann organized an evening in honor of Buber and
invited me to participate, and that was when I got to
know Buber better. At that meeting Buber lectured
in German and I translated into Hebrew. Afterward I
traveled with him to Beit Alpha, where he also lectured and I translated his lecture into Hebrew. After
Buber came to Israel in 1939 I started meeting with
him more regularly. I remember that he had some
fears about how well he would master the Hebrew
language.

Q. Can you give an example of those fears?

A. Partially. You see, Buber was then bringing out his
book of Hasidic tales in Hebrew, and he wasn't sure
of the Hebrew, so he asked me to go through the proofs
and correct them, and also to comment on the Hebrew. But he told me, "Although I am a rich man I
do not have money to pay you, since all my money
remained in Germany." I told Buber that I would be
happy to assist him without getting paid. He was surprised and asked why. I told him that I felt I owed
him something, and reminded him of his helping me
out of my loneliness at the youth village near Vienna.

Q. How was it to work with Buber?

A. I worked with him more than a year on correcting the
proofs of his Hasidic tales. It was nice. Usually the
author tries to get things to move quickly, he hurries

people along. Buber did not hurry me along. He would
listen when I criticized him and would nod his head
in agreement or disagreement. He had great patience
and would hear my criticisms patiently, at times saying, "You are right." I was younger than he was by
quite a bit and it was as if he was a teacher-friend. I
never felt that he was looking down at me, and if he
had comments he would state them in such a way that
I could learn from him. In general, when a person met
with him, Buber conveyed the feeling that he had
made you into one of his students. During this period
I learned that Buber's writings had little to do with
his way of life.

Q. Can you give examples of the gap between his writings and his life?

A. I remember two examples that I believe are indica-
tive. The first was when Buber came to me to work
on his book on the eve of Yom Kippur. I was astounded and asked him if he didn't know that today
was the eve of Yom Kippur. He answered that he knew
and asked me if I kept the fast and the holy day. I
nodded yes. Buber got up and said, "If you keep the
Mitzvoth, then I'll leave. Keep them." It was difficult
for me to understand that Buber, who wrote about
nurturing our relation to our tradition, did not keep
the tradition himself. The second incident occurred
when I was working with him in his study. A woman
came to the door and in German asked Buber for charity. He got very angry at her and yelled, "Get out of
here. Get out, get out!" Afterward I turned to Buber
and asked him, "How can it be that you, who write
so beautifully about being charitable, yell at a woman
who comes to you to beg for charity?" He answered:

"Nu, what can I do, I can't stand it." I want to stress that Buber responded to that woman without a bit of grace, he was simply aggressive.

Q. How did you feel when you finished working with Buber on that book?

A. That brings to mind another incident. After the book was published, Buber brought me three copies as a present, and he wrote a very short terse dedication in each book. That cold dedication made me very angry. It had no mention of the amount of hours and work I had put into the book. When I read it I was so angry that to his face I tore the page with the dedication out of the book.

Q. How did Buber respond?

A. Buber didn't answer, but he blushed. I believe that Buber had a problem here. He refused to give another person the feeling of satisfaction that that person had helped him.

Q. Was that the end of your relationship?

A. No, not at all. Afterward I did the proofreading of *Gog und Magog* in Hebrew [*For the Sake of Heaven* in English], but I was paid by the publisher. After these incidents Buber would meet with me as a friend. He was faithful to me, despite the incident. And I must say that it was pleasant to walk with Buber and talk with him. I gladly assumed the role of the disciple, and was happy to let him assume the role of the great teacher. He was an extremely bright person.

Q. How was the atmosphere when you worked together?

A. There was no tension; Buber spoke quietly, in a peaceful manner.

Q. Did Buber have a sense of humor?

A. He had a great sense of humor and laughed heartily when you told him a joke.

Q. What were your impressions of the works you proof-read, and did you share these impressions with Buber?

A. One of my impressions was that Buber often slightly changed the Hasidic stories that he retold so that they would be more palatable to his readers, and to his own views on mysticism. I told him this about specific stories, like the well-known story of the young boy who whistles in synagogue on Yom Kippur. Buber always answered that he had found a source with the version that he was printing. I'm skeptical.

Q. Did Buber ever speak to you about his childhood?

A. Never. He always wanted to appear perfect. I also never felt that any significant relationship existed between Buber and his children. He spoke about them as if they were strangers.

Q. Were you ever at a meeting between Buber and his children?

A. No, but I heard him speak of them.

Q. Did you continue to come to Buber's house after you stopped working together?

A. Only for special occasions, such as when a party was held by the writers' union for one of its members and Buber spoke. When he spoke he assumed a pose, and he knew how to play with rhetoric. But when he walked with me, I don't think he assumed a pose.

Q. Did you meet with Paula, Buber's wife?

A. Yes, my impression was that there was great love between them. But she was also an actor.

Q. What else do you remember from your meetings with Buber?

A. When Buber was honored, he was never surprised at the honors he received. For instance, after I read his book on Rabbi Nachman, I told him, "If I felt that this were a good book, I'd have been happy to translate it into Hebrew." He agreed with my evaluation and said, "Look, I wrote the book when I was eighteen years old, what do you want?" But when an English publisher offered him a large sum of money to have that book translated into English, he immediately agreed. Buber was fond of money. When, after the Holocaust, he was offered the German Peace Prize, he immediately accepted it. I believe that if he wanted to open dialogue with the Germans, he could have gone and accepted the prize, but given away the money, or refused it. But Buber was too fond of money. Despite all this I felt comfortable with him and could borrow something I needed from him, even though I was not one of his students and did not adhere to his political approaches.

Interview with Kalman Yaron

(Student of Buber. He is currently manager of Martin Buber Center in Jerusalem.)

Q. How did you get to know Buber?

A. I was a student at the Seminar for National Teachers at which Buber was the figurehead, although Gideon Freudenberg was the person in charge. Buber seemed to have thought about establishing the Seminar in order to teach all the illiterate adults who arrived in Israel immediately after the War of Independence. But Buber was active only in the background. We only met him when he came to teach.

Q. How was he as a teacher?

A. Not that interesting. He taught us the book of Amos from the Bible. I don't believe that any of us felt that his lectures were exciting. They were not an attempt to reach a dialogue, but rather a long monologue. There were very few questions from the students, and I would hold that Buber did not realize his dialogical philosophy in our class. Dialogue can develop in the classroom, I believe, if genuine questions are asked; but Buber did not ask genuine questions. And I don't believe that his manner of presentation encouraged us to ask genuine questions. He did try to show us the humanistic aspects of the Bible, like "Love your neighbor as you love yourself."

Q. So, Buber did not realize his dialogical philosophy as a teacher?

A. The only incident that I remember where he might have realized dialogue was when we came to the personal interview to be accepted at the Seminar. Buber tried to develop a dialogue with the person he was interviewing. He asked me about my work with newcomers to Israel and the conversation was a dialogue. Buber listened and responded. But his philosophy did not influence the Seminar. Buber was a practical person, and my impression is that he knew how to use his fame to establish the Seminar. I felt his practicality even in the few encounters I had with him.

First Interview with Ernst Simon

(Professor Emeritus of Education at
Hebrew Univ. in Jerusalem)

Q. Do you believe that Martin Buber personally realized his educational approach?

A. I'd like to make a comment about the question; I'm not sure that the possibility of realizing an educational approach is linked to its realization by the person who originated that approach. I believe that Pestalozzi's educational method succeeded only when other people adopted it, not when he himself attempted to realize it. A better formulation of the question might be whether there are hints in Buber's life that might assist us to realize his educational approach.

Q. Would you feel more comfortable if I asked whether Buber realized his philosophy of personal relations as a father, grandfather, teacher, educator?

A. I think that this question is even more off base. It is much more difficult to realize a philosophy or an approach with people who are closer to you. Emotional involvement, day-to-day closeness, high expectations and similar attitudes can make one despise a specific educational approach. I know that Buber taught his children at home, he did not send them to school. I believe that that was a mistake, even though it was an attempt to realize his educational approach. Through this decision he took from his children the experience of living and growing up together with other children. I believe that it was different when his granddaughters grew up in his house.

Q. Do you think that Buber was sensitive to the fact that

his granddaughters came to him after their parents were divorced?

A. I don't know. I think the relations were good. They called him PapaMartin.

Q. How was Buber as a teacher?

A. Buber was rarely a teacher, at least until he came to Israel and became a professor at Hebrew University. Later he taught at the Seminar for National Teachers.

Q. What about his teaching at the *Lehrhaus* in Frankfurt?

A. I wrote to him once, after hearing one of his lectures there, how poorly that lecture was organized and how insensitive Buber was to his listeners. My letter appears on page 172 of the second volume of his published correspondence in German. I believe that Buber was open to criticism of the kind that I brought up. He didn't answer in writing because he had an opportunity to speak.

Q. Was Buber always open to criticism?

A. I believe he was. For instance, he was very patient with Gershom Scholem. When they organized an Academic Evening to celebrate Scholem's sixtieth birthday, I spoke and opened with something that Buber once told me. Buber said, "Each one of us has students; some of them establish a scholarly approach. One of my students created a scholarly field; that student is Scholem." I believe that Buber's saying something like that about Scholem, who constantly criticized him, reveals that Buber was open to criticism.

Q. Wasn't Scholem's main criticism of Buber in the field of Hasidism?

A. Yes, but it went to the heart of Buber's spirituality. And Buber spent over half a century researching Hasidism. I once made a mistake. I told Buber that Scholem had praised *Gog und Magog* [*For the Sake of Heaven*, in English]. Buber answered: "Yes, but I know exactly why he praised it." Buber knew that Scholem appreciated him as a storyteller, and had praised the story Buber told in that book. But he did not believe that Buber had presented the essence of Hasidism. Since Buber was willing to accept criticism from students, some of them later became friends. Buber always behaved with composure. He also had persons who hated him.

Q. For instance?

A. I don't want to mention names. I wouldn't want to contribute to the anti-Buberian atmosphere prevailing now in Israel. I can think of people whose disappointment with him became a strong feeling.

Q. Did Buber ever attempt to call one of these disappointed persons and speak to him or to her?

A. I'm not sure that he was conscious of the fact that these people were disappointed with him. But Buber did criticize himself in some of his writings, so he knew that, at times, he didn't succeed. There was a reason for his disappointing people. He was a religious Jew who did not keep the Mitzvoth, he was a Zionist who for sixty years criticized certain Zionist approaches. He was not understood by those persons who wished to place him in a certain category and couldn't. This lack of specificity was also a weakness that appeared in his writings. When the reader was waiting for Buber to give him an example of his thought, he offered an epigram or an analogy.

Q. How was Buber as an academic teacher?

A. I don't believe he succeeded. He had few students; many were very unhappy with him as a teacher. He taught without a method. A teacher needs a method if he wants to succeed. Even a great impression cannot take the place of a method. I believe that to some extent Buber did succeed in the Seminar for National Teachers.

Q. In your conversations with him, or in his conversations with his students, did Buber ever give personal examples?

A. Not many, and perhaps it was better that way.

Q. Was Buber ever skeptical about the possibility of realizing his philosophy?

A. No, he really believed in it.

Q. How would Buber go about realizing his philosophy in a school? If Buber had been given the opportunity to set up a school guided by his philosophy, what would he have done?

A. Create a therapeutic atmosphere. In love, you can be hurt when your loved one says something that hurts. In education, this should never occur. You must always see an attempt to hurt you as a symptom that points to a problem that needs to be dealt with.

Q. Do you have anything to add?

A. Perhaps I should tell you about my first meeting with Buber, which took place shortly after the First World War. I had submitted an article to the journal *Der Jude*, which Buber edited. Buber responded by inviting me to visit him at his home. After we had conversed for a while, Buber mentioned my article and added, "It's a fine article and I will be happy to publish it, but it contains one clause that makes me feel uncomfortable. You draw a parallel between the Biblical Balaam and the Jewish historian Dubnow, saying that they both wanted to curse, but they expressed a blessing. I feel unhappy with that comparison: Dubnow was an important Jewish scholar while Balaam was a Mesopotamian diviner who served Israel's enemy. Would you agree to change the text?" I, of course, agreed, but what impressed me was that Buber had chosen to discuss such a change in a face-to-face meeting.

Second Interview with Ernst Simon

Q. What were the relations between Buber and Ben Gurion?

A. They met at times and had violent arguments. They seemed to be speaking different languages. Ben Gurion appreciated Buber's fame in the world. But at times they reached grave disagreements, even vicious disagreements, as when Buber stood up for Aharon Cohen, whom Ben Gurion wanted brought to trial and condemned. I also wrote to Ben Gurion on this topic, and he responded viciously. Buber and Ben Gurion had different scales of values, and they used a different language. Ben Gurion always spoke in political and national terms, and Buber did not appreciate these terms. I personally believe that Ben Gurion's language has become the basis for the rightwing fanaticism that we see today in Israel.

Q. Did Buber have any relations with Arabs, for instance through Brith Shalom?

A. I believe that we were good at justifying links with Arabs on the philosophical level, Buber, Magnus, myself, and others, but we did not translate what we were saying to a language that the ordinary person could understand. Neither did we make an attempt to build relationships with Arabs. For instance, we never learned Arabic. Buber did participate in international meetings, held at Florence, where he met Prince Hassan of Morocco and did develop a sort of dialogue with him. But I don't believe that Buber did much to bring the dialogical principle into politics. Hassan has meanwhile become king of Morocco.

Q. How was Buber during his last years? Did he become senile?

A. No, he was very clearheaded until the age of 85. After that it was difficult for him to concentrate. I remember him saying as he grew older: "I have only one prayer to God, that he won't take my spiritual integrity from me as I grow older."

Q. Why was Buber not understood here in Israel?

A. One reason was that he spoke in a language that he had created and simple people did not understand that language. He also did not conform to a specific creed, even if he believed in something. For instance, Buber believed in God but did not keep the Mizvoth; even on Yom Kippur he didn't fast. I believe that the mediocre intellectual in Israel did not accept Buber, because Buber defied a specific labeling. He was accepted, though, by Christians.

Q. So, Buber had no relations with Arabs beyond what you mentioned?

A. There were some meetings with Atalla Mansour, who is now a journalist for *Haaretz*. He met with Buber, and there are letters from him to Buber in the third volume of the Buber correspondence. Mansour said, and wrote, to Buber that in the political situation in which he found himself, he hesitated to get married. Buber encouraged him to get married. He also met with an Arab Christian Archbishop from Syria or Lebanon. When he spoke to me about that meeting, Buber called the Archbishop an old fox. The meetings did not continue.

Q. Did Buber have a sense of humor?

A. I wouldn't say that Buber had a sense of humor. His personality was characterized by pathos. He celebrated pathos, and that distanced him from young people.

Interview with Eliezer Beeri

(Beeri got to know Buber through his granddaughters. He later was a member of Kibbutz Hazorea.)

Q. When did you first get to know Buber?

A. In Heppenheim in the 1930s. My sister was the counselor of his granddaughters. Later I would visit him about three to four times a year in Jerusalem.

Q. Did you feel welcome in his house?

A. Yes. When I arrived in Jerusalem from the kibbutz, I'd often call and ask if we could meet. Buber always invited me. I liked to hear his wisdom. He knew so much in so many fields. Once he told me that nothing interested him more than modern physics.

Q. Did he ask you about yourself?

A. Of course. He'd ask about the kibbutz. As you know, my kibbutz, Kibbutz Hazorea, was established by people who identified themselves as students of Buber. He always wanted to hear about the kibbutz. He would often begin our conversation with the question, "What is bothering you?" I would begin to answer and the conversation would flow.

Q. What were the topics you talked about most?

A. Besides the kibbutz, we talked a lot about politics. Buber was very angry at the way Ben Gurion was leading the country. He wanted much more stress on human relations, and less stress on power politics. I remember not agreeing with Buber's stressing that the Jews were to blame for the way our relations developed with our Arab neighbors.

Q. Did you feel comfortable at Buber's house?

A. Not always. Buber was very affluent; money was very important to him. He knew how to take care of his property. His way of life was simple, but in his home were many beautiful pieces of art and utensils. When I came we would converse in his study. He would sit behind his desk, and I in front of the desk facing him. He never invited me to eat anything at his home. He never offered me a cup of coffee. At times, in the middle of a conversation, his wife would enter and say: "Martin, now it is time for your coffee." And then, nothing else could be done. He would go drink his coffee in the kitchen—without ever suggesting that I join him—and return after a while. . . . On second thought, perhaps once or twice over the years, I was offered a cup of coffee; I don't remember that well. Those times were definitely exceptions. I don't think he ever drank near me and did not offer me a cup of coffee. He usually just went to the kitchen alone and drank his coffee there, leaving me alone in his study.

Q. I understand that Buber never visited Kibbutz Hazorea, even though it was established by people who called themselves his followers. Why?

A. At first there was a cooling-off period in our relations with Buber. He disappointed us. In the early 1930s we went to Israel and he remained in Heppenheim. Here was a person who had argued with Herzl about the realization of Zionism, but who chose to sit in Heppenheim until 1937. We felt that our ways had parted. I suspect that Buber felt that also. In addition, he severely criticized the kibbutz movement and the strict adherence to political parties that characterized us during that period. He believed that a political party should arise to realize a specific idea. But he perceived that party administrations started to rule political parties merely to further their own interests, and he rejected such an approach. Later, when we renewed our relations with Buber, I would answer that as long as there is no better way of organizing political action, parties are the best means we have. And Buber never suggested any other kind of political action; he just criticized political parties.

Q. When the relations were renewed, after the cooling-off period, did you relate to Buber more as a peer?

A. Not really, but we did point out where we disagreed with him. And he accepted it. "You go your way, and I'll go mine," was his answer. I admire Buber, but I do not think that we should relate to him as a hero of Judaism. Buber made mistakes. He made grave mistakes, in my view, in his evaluation of the kibbutz movement, and when he pointed out that the ideals we had embraced had been disappointing. When he wrote that, I responded with a stiff letter to him and asked, "How do you know?" He answered, "As long as I still breathe, I will know what is happening in this land."

Q. These disagreements did not interfere in your relations?

A. Not at all. When Menachem Gerson and I came to congratulate Buber on his 75th birthday, he told us that there was a proposal to plant a forest in his name, and that he would like it to be planted near Kibbutz Hazorea. Buber was not a modest person. He knew his worth. He asked me, "What do you think?" I was very excited, and of course we both agreed.

Q. Why didn't he visit Hazorea after the relations warmed up again?

A. In his later years he seldom traveled. He once told me that he had gone to a concert in Jerusalem and that it had been very difficult for him. In those years when I would ask him how he felt, he would precisely enumerate all the places in his body where he had pains or health problems. He would talk about his health very seriously. Still, he flew to Switzerland a couple of times. I asked him, "Is Kibbutz Hazorea farther than Switzerland?" He answered, "They take me to Switzerland, I don't have to make any effort." I believe he had inner inhibitions. He may have feared that he'd get too excited, or meet some people who did not appreciate him. Once he was on vacation in Nazareth and had agreed to come. But on that day a telegram arrived saying that Buber was ill and had returned to Jerusalem.

Q. Did Buber ever discuss ugly things with you?

A. Of course. He did not see everything through the eyes of an aesthete. He spoke of difficult things that happened to him during his life, like his health problems, or problems of his son Raphael's wife. Many times he expressed strong criticisms to people or about people.

Q. You were with Buber in the Jewish-Arab Friendship League. Did Buber have any close relations with Arabs?

A. He always supported a political agreement with them. Until the War of Independence of 1948, he lived in an Arab neighborhood of Jerusalem, and would at times visit Arabs there. But no, despite his pro-Arab, pro-dialogue views, as far as I know, Buber hardly ever met with Arabs.

Interview with Fania Scholem
(Gershom Scholem's wife)

(She was married to Gershom Scholem, who had a long association with Buber that ended with some bitter criticisms of him.)

Q. What was your relationship to Buber?

A. It was complex. On the one hand we admired him, but on the other hand we were very critical. It was the little things that peeved us, like his holding that Jews must renew their relation to the Jewish tradition, and then people coming to his house in Heppenheim on Saturday and seeing the cleaning being done on Shabat—so that on Sunday the house would be clean. Or his demanding Jewish-Arab dialogue and then making his home in a house that Arab refugees had left behind when they fled Jerusalem.

Q. Did you like meeting with Buber?

A. It was a pleasure—when Buber was alone. I enjoyed hearing his wisdom, I would joke with him, show chutzpah, tell him what was on my mind. But when other people appeared he started acting like a prophet. I liked his intuition, it reminded me of a cat or a tiger. He also helped me a lot when I was working for the freeing of Russian Jews. He sent telegrams and let me use his name.

Q. How did you get to know Buber?

A. Through my husband, who knew him in Germany. When we became friends, Buber would visit me, even when my husband was not at home. When Gershom and I got married, Buber took me to the open market and taught me how to buy. He had a tremendous craving for sweets, and when we returned from the market he would always buy himself ice cream. He usually took himself too seriously, and lacked a spontaneous sense of humor, but since I was very straightforward with him, and often responded humorously, he got along with me. Of course, I did not ask him personal questions or discuss personal problems—after all there was a 35-year difference in our ages. But we usually got along splendidly, and someone told me that before his death he said that I was one of his best friends here in Israel.

Q. Did you go to hear his lectures?

A. No, and I'm glad I didn't, because I learned much more from our friendly relationship. Once, when I was a student, Professor Hugo Bergmann invited the philosophy students to a discussion with Buber. Buber spoke and we were enchanted. Late at night we left the house and started walking home together. Suddenly we stopped in the middle of the road and asked ourselves: What in the world had Buber said?—Not one of us could answer.

Q. So, you felt comfortable visiting him at his home?

A. Very. Even when he was sick, and even after my husband wrote very strong criticisms of Buber's work on Hasidism, Buber always acted like a gentleman and did not let these arguments interfere with our relationship. Once when he was ill he called and asked me to come visit him. My husband accompanied me and then I saw that Buber felt uncomfortable. He would have preferred me to come alone. Perhaps my husband's being strong and healthy made him feel uncomfortable.

Q. After that, did you go alone to visit him?

A. No. I didn't want to come with my husband and make Buber feel uncomfortable, and I didn't want to go without my husband knowing that I went. And my husband did not seem to like it when I went alone. So I didn't go. I did visit him again a few weeks before he died. My husband went with me then, too.

Q. Was there always tension between your husband and Buber?

A. No, not at all. My husband was nineteen years old when he first met Buber, who immediately appreciated his talents. Paula Buber also appreciated my husband and said that he would be an important man. I believe that my husband started being critical of Buber when Buber did not practice what he preached. He sent his students from Germany to Palestine to establish Kibbutz Hazorea, while he remained in Heppenheim.

Q. Were you bothered by the age difference between you and Buber?

A. Not at all. He was a very lively person, his life was vivacious, and hence I felt that I could always learn from him. His being lively might have been the reason he liked my chutzpah and straightforwardness. I was attracted to his liveliness and to all that I could learn from him.

Q. What were your relations with Paula?

A. She was not rooted in what was occurring in Israel, and she spent much time writing. My relationship was with Buber, not with her.

Q. Was Buber a good host?

A. Not really. He seemed happy when someone visited him, but he never offered his visitor anything to eat or to drink. I remember once, when I was visiting him on a very hot day, an elderly visitor entered. Buber received him nicely, but he didn't even offer the old man a glass of water, even though it was terribly hot outside. I believe that Buber simply did not think of these things.

Q. From what you say, it seems that Buber lived a life of solitude.

A. Yes, but that is what he wanted.

Interview with Benyamin Uffenheimer
(Professor of Biblical Studies at Tel Aviv Univ.)

Q. When did you first hear about Buber?

A. I grew up in a small town in Germany and attended secondary school during the years that Hitler came to power. In 1934–35, a group of Jewish students from Freiburg reached our town and started speaking with the young people about Zionism. They were traveling through all the small towns, bringing the message of Zionism to the Jews. That was when I first heard the name Martin Buber, and at the age of 16 I started reading his books. They enchanted me, and moved me so deeply that I could never finish a book—it aroused such a storm of emotions in me. Buber's writings were for me a response to Nazi propaganda. They helped me decide to leave Germany and come to Israel—I had no Zionist education at home. When I was in Hachshara [training camp to come to Israel] we would read Buber together. We read him as a great teacher.

Q. When did you first meet Buber?

A. When I studied at the Hebrew University in the early 1940s, he taught sociology of civilization, and I took some of his courses.

Q. Was he a good teacher?

A. Not really. As a teacher there is little to tell about him. His lectures were quite mediocre. It seemed that he was basically involved in his own research and writing. It was often difficult to follow his lectures. There was no conversation or dialogue in the classroom, even though there were few students. Buber read from his notes and we tried to follow. In the seminars it was a little better, but not much. We read together the writings of French Utopian writers. Buber tried to develop discussions, free discussions, and he didn't mind being attacked. I remember a woman who took the class who was a communist; she often attacked his views. He would smile, stroke his beard, try to understand her and relate her arguments to what appeared in the text. He never got angry. His seminars were more lively than many other seminars that were downright boring. During this period I started studying the Bible and Buber was, in my view, a representative of the approach that does not limit itself to solving linguistic and technical historical problems. He strove to get to the inner essence of problems in a Biblical text. Again, I was enchanted.

Q. Did Buber keep a distance from his students?

A. In those days he didn't need to keep a distance, since it was normal for there to be a distance between teacher and student. Most of us came from Europe, where distance between student and teacher was natural. If you wanted to discuss something with Buber you could always set up a meeting with him, and come to his home. But from what I know, these meetings never became intimate. Perhaps here Buber was to blame.

Q. Did Buber ever ask you about your problems?

A. No, Buber always kept a distance.

Q. After completing your studies, did you keep up your connection with Buber?

A. In a roundabout manner. When he lectured on Genesis at *Emet Veemuna* synagogue, I attended. When he lectured on Amos and other prophets at a Youth Aliyah seminar, I attended. I did not accept Buber's political views, but his writings and lectures on the Bible have influenced me deeply, both as a teacher and as a professor of Bible at Tel Aviv University where I am doing research in this field. In general, although he was a weak teacher, Buber contributed a great deal to the curriculum of the Hebrew University by teaching those philosophers who were central to German sociology, something that is hardly taught now when experimental sociology reigns.

Q. After you were no longer his student, did Buber make you feel more comfortable when you met with him?

A. No. It was hard to approach him. Perhaps it was because I was young, but he also did not open himself. He was congenial, but I do not think that he wanted to become close to people. I believe that he was much too enchanted with himself and so concerned with his work and writing that he didn't want to dedicate time to other people. I believe that is the reason he also refused to take part in the public life of the university by running for and accepting a role in running the university, such as dean or rector. I met with Buber again when I taught at the school for teachers of the nation. Buber was the educational figure in the background, but he still kept a distance. Gideon Freudenberg did the work and Buber was the figurehead in charge. This was in the 1950s. At times Buber taught there, but I do not know whether he taught well.

Q. I understand that after this period you hardly met with him.

A. True. On his eightieth birthday I was invited to speak in his honor. I was deeply impressed by him then. After the meeting I was invited to his home and we spoke more personally, but he didn't open up much. At the dinner following the celebration Agnon and Scholem spoke. Buber answered Scholem with humor and did not remain in debt—he responded to all of Scholem's criticisms, but with humor. When Buber completed his translation of the Bible, I was again invited to speak in his honor, and I pointed out some of the approaches that Buber had developed to translating the Bible. This occurred in 1962. I was again very impressed by Buber. He read a section of his translation, and he read very beautifully. He always knew how to look aesthetically, so that he never gave you the impression that he was aged. He was open to criticism, at least ready to listen. When a person asked him, "Is this your opinion?" He would often answer: "I don't have opinions, I'm merely pointing to the truth."

Q. You mentioned Buber's humor; do you mean to say that he had a sense of humor?

A. If he did, I hardly ever encountered it. He never joked. At times he was sarcastic, but never toward his pupils. At times he would attack Ben Gurion in this manner. I remember that on Buber's eightieth birthday, Ben Gurion sat in the first row of the audience, while Buber sat at the head table with a picture of Herzl on the wall behind him. When Buber was called upon to speak, he recalled that after being the editor of *Die Welt* [the first periodical of the Zionist movement] for a year, in 1904 he decided to resign. Herzl asked him to please continue, but Buber refused. And Buber added, "I refused because the spirit should not surrender to a statesman."

First Interview with Moshe Shpitzer

(An editor and publisher. He served as Buber's secretary in 1932–34.)

Q. When did you first encounter Buber?

A. I was born in Czechoslovakia, in Moravia, in 1900, to a Zionist family that was also traditional. During the First World War I read Buber's book on Rabbi Nachman. In 1916 Buber came out with his journal *Der Jude*, which greatly impressed me. I started to write to Buber and he answered me. I was the only Jew in my high school class and I was seeking contacts with other Jews.

Q. Do you remember your first meeting with Buber?

A. No, I don't. As far as I recall it was at a convention of Poale Zion in Prague, but I don't remember details. I do remember that I saw him during the 1920s, and that in 1928 I was editor of a Zionist periodical called *Hanoar*, which led me to renew contacts with Buber. The first issue of that periodical appeared on February 8, 1928, on Buber's fiftieth birthday. I wrote an open letter to him in that first issue, and when I sent him a copy of the issue I wrote him a more personal letter. The first meetings with Buber that I clearly remember occurred a bit later, when I was head of an educational institute for Jewish youth at which Zionists and non-Zionists studied together. It was a sort of open school; lecturers came from different backgrounds. Buber came and gave a series of lectures on the Bible. Hundreds of people participated in these lectures. During that period our relationship became more personal.

Q. I understand that you worked with Buber for a while as his assistant. How did that come about?

A. I was living in Berlin, and in addition to managing
the educational institute that I mentioned, I was
teaching the children of Schocken, the head of the famous Jewish publishing company. I wanted to leave
Berlin in order to separate myself from a certain
woman. I had a friend in Berlin called Lambert
Schneider. He was a publisher, and he initiated the
idea of having Buber translate the Bible. Things became difficult with this publication when Rosenzweig
died. In addition, people weren't buying the Bible,
and Lambert Schneider was on the verge of bank-
ruptcy. He went to Leo Baeck, who was head of the
German Jewish community, and Baeck decided to buy
7000 copies of the Buber/Rosenzweig translation of
the Torah for Bnai Brith. This decision saved Lambert
Schneider, but he still had to sell out. Leo Baeck
suggested to Lambert Schneider that he approach
Schocken and work out a deal with him. Schocken
was interested in Jewish culture and was willing to
invest money in these areas. When Lambert Schneider
came to him, Schocken's response was, "I've been
waiting for you for many years." Schocken was impressed that Lambert Schneider, a Christian, could be
interested in Jewish culture. Schocken bought up all
of Lambert Schneider's Jewish works, and especially
the Buber/Rosenzweig Bible translation. Lambert
Schneider agreed to this buyout under the condition
that he would continue managing these works at
Schocken's publishing house. Schocken also agreed to
continue the Buber/Rosenzweig Bible translation.
They set up a meeting with Buber, and Buber agreed
to continue but he said he needed some help. Lambert
Schneider knew that I wanted to get out of Berlin
and suggested that I be offered the job. So on May 1,

1932, I reached Heppenheim to start working with Buber.

Q. What did you do?

A. I helped Buber mainly in two fields. I went through the proofs and commented on anything that seemed wrong, including what I thought Buber had done wrong. And I gathered material for Buber on the specific book that he was translating. I remember gathering much material for his translation of the Psalms. I summarized some of the relevant articles. In addition I would write letters for Buber. I was in charge of answering letters written to him by women.

Q. Did Buber accept your comments?

A. Yes, I must say that Buber responded cordially to all of my comments. He listened carefully.

Q. Why did Buber have you respond, in his name, to letters written to him by women?

A. I don't know. Among them were many high society women; some of them seeking a way back to Judaism. Buber became well known in these circles after Hitler came to power and he started teaching at the Frankfurt *Lehrhaus*.

Q. How was Buber as a teacher?

A. I often accompanied Buber to his lectures at Frankfurt University. He was a very poor teacher. I told him that since he only sat up there on the stage and talked, his message was not reaching his students. I suggested that he try and sit closer to his students and that he relate to them. Afterward when he taught at the *Lehrhaus*, he was much better. After Hitler came to power, the Jews were seeking for a message like the one that Buber was conveying—that there is a way back to Judaism—and many came to hear him. He received many letters from students. I answered many of these letters, especially those written by women.

Q. How did Buber respond when people approached him?

A. He was open, but he had to protect himself because at that time many people wanted to consult him. I myself consulted him when that woman I had separated myself from came to Heppenheim.

Q. Do you remember any significant incident when Buber was open to another person?

A. I remember one interesting incident. On May 1, 1933, we were sitting in Buber's house in Heppenheim. It was very hot. There was a May Day parade organized by the Nazis, and since the windows were open we saw and heard parts of it. After the parade ended, a maid came to Buber and said that a man wanted to speak to him. They went into Buber's study, and after a few minutes the young man left. Buber emerged from his study very excited. He said that the young man was an employee of the government and had been ordered to participate in the parade. It had made him disgusted with himself, and he felt that he couldn't come home to his wife and child without expressing this disgust to Buber. He said to Buber, "I lifted my hand to say Heil Hitler and I feel that the hand is filthy. Please shake my hand and I promise that I will never again raise my hand in such a salute." We later learned that he resigned from his government post, and opened a private firm as a lawyer. His name is Ludwig Metzger. After the war he became mayor of Darmstadt and was also a member of the Bundestag and was active in support of Israel.

Q. How was Buber as an employer?

A. He always gave and demanded respect. He was quite

open and I felt free, even though he did not invite me into his family circle. I never ate at his house, but I did join him and his wife for walks at times. I taught his granddaughters Hebrew, and to this day I'm in contact with them.

Q. How long did you work with Buber?

A. From May 1, 1932, until October 1934. Afterward I was still in contact with him because I worked at Schocken's publishing house in Berlin.

Q. Why did you stop working with Buber?

A. Buber no longer needed someone with literary abilities for his translation; he felt that he needed someone who would help him organize the work, and I was not interested in that kind of employment. I preferred literary work, and Schocken was willing to give me a long-term contract.

Q. Did Buber ever speak to you about his childhood?

A. No, never.

Q. Do you recall any significant encounters with Buber?

A. A few. One of them had to do with Buber's relationship to Yom Kippur. There was a small synagogue in Heppenheim with a very small congregation. The synagogue was built with the help of a contribution from a Jew from Heppenheim who had gone to America and become rich. On the eve of Yom Kippur, 1932, a friend came to visit me and we went together to that synagogue. Buber did not go. When the time for praying arrived, there was not a minyan and we had to ask non-Jews who were passing by to come in for a short time so that we could pray. My friend and I felt uncomfortable about such a manner of praying, and the next day we decided to walk five kilometers, even though we were fasting, to another village where there were sure to be enough Jews to pray together.

It was a nice synagogue with a warm atmosphere, and we spent the entire day there, in the synagogue, praying. In front of us sat an old man, and after the prayer he asked us if we had relatives in the village; when we said we didn't he invited us to break the fast in his home. We were a bit hesitant, but he told us that we had a long way to walk and should eat before that. So we went to his home with him after the prayers. When we came in we noticed that the old man had an elderly unmarried daughter, and that he was very poor. We sat and ate and talked a bit. When the old man heard that I worked for Buber, he said, "They say that Buber does not fast on Yom Kippur." I asked him, "What is the difference between not keeping Yom Kippur and not keeping the Sabbath?" He answered, "According to the Halachah there is no difference, but according to tradition there is." When I told Buber about this encounter it shocked him. He became very defensive and said, "Every year when Yom Kippur comes around it is more difficult for me not to keep the fast than to keep it." He then added, "Don't think that my wife influences me to not keep the fast. In fact, she suggested that I keep it." I know that after Hitler came to power, Buber made an exception and on Passover he went to the synagogue, and gave a sermon there.

Q. Did Buber have a sense of humor?

A. I would not say that he had a sense of humor, but he did like to tell jokes.

Q. Do you recall any other significant incident?

A. When Buber taught at the Jewish *Lehrhaus* in Frankfurt, after Hitler came to power, many gentiles came to the lectures, in addition to the Jews. Among them was a Catholic called Ernst Michel, who had been manager of the Academy of Labor, but was dismissed because he refused to swear allegiance to Hitler. After he was dismissed he traveled from town to town and lectured to priests. One day Buber was very tense because he had received a letter from Michel. He said to me, "I'll let you see the letter, but tell no one about it." I agreed. Michel had written, "After hearing your lectures I see that I am really a Jew and not a Christian. I don't know if now is the time to do something about it." A few days later as I was walking in Frankfurt I met Michel. He immediately asked me, "Did you read my letter?" I was astounded and did not reply. I did not tell Buber about this incident. I only wondered.

Q. How did people relate to Buber in Heppenheim?

A. He did not walk much around the town. He would only go to the post office. He had a weird habit of reading while he walked. They used to say: "Professor Buber thinks even when he walks."

Second Interview with Moshe Shpitzer

Q. Was Buber active politically during the period you were working for him? After all, those years were an eventful and difficult period.

A. No, Buber was not active in politics. He was active in the cultural field; he was attempting to help Jews attain knowledge about their heritage, and pride in that heritage. He did have links with people who were active politically, like Baeck and Warbourg.

Q. Were you active politically?

A. No. How could one be active politically when such activities were against the law? The leadership of the Jewish community was in the hands of people who had to balance their steps between the needs of the community and the existing possibilities and exigencies. They went as far as possible without risking the destruction of the community. Leo Baeck was a very brave person who did such a balancing act. He told me that once the Gestapo wanted him to fire one of his subordinates. He refused and told the Gestapo: "You can torture me, hit me, and maybe even make my hand sign a document firing that man. But you can't make me be president of the Jewish community after that man has been fired." Remember, Baeck was an old man, alone since his wife had died, but very courageous.

Q. Did Buber express his views in public?

A. Mainly by writing articles that could be understood as criticizing the regime, even though their topic may have been something different.

Q. Was he influential?

A. I think he was. He had people working with him who spread his views. He himself traveled to many places to lecture, even though he was already fifty-five years old. He was committed and dedicated. Many simple uneducated people came to hear him and were influenced. Some of his listeners later became active in Jewish affairs. He also influenced non-Jews who listened to him.

Q. Why did Buber ask you to respond to the women who wrote to him?

A. He was busy. But I think he also feared that perhaps these women might interfere with his family life. He was afraid that they might want to visit him at his home. These were women who, when Hitler came to power, were shocked, and sought a way back to Judaism. They wanted assistance. Perhaps Buber also thought that I could help them.

Q. Did you keep contact with Buber after you both came to Israel?

A. Yes, we were in contact over the years and would visit each other. In the hospital when he was already dying he told me: "Shpitzer, we should have met each other more often." Since he didn't want to remain in the hospital, and he was Martin Buber, the doctors let him return home to die.

Q. How did Buber receive guests?

A. In Heppenheim there were few, since it was a small out-of-the-way place, and when people came Mrs. Buber took care of them—but only if she was acquainted with them. She would bring coffee and cakes. If she didn't know the people she would ignore them. Buber never offered his guests anything to eat or to drink. If something was offered, it was by Mrs. Buber. At most he would offer a book of his if he felt a need to give something to a guest. That manner of receiving people continued after the Bubers moved to Jerusalem.

Q. What were your impressions of the relations between Buber and Paula?

A. They were good, but I probably should add that she could be a rather strongheaded woman. I remember once when the three of us were riding on a train together, Buber showed her a copy he had received that morning of a new book of his. In it he had written a dedication to her, presumably without her permission. She got very angry and scolded him right there, in the train compartment, and made him promise that the dedication would not appear in subsequent editions. She did all this with me present, without qualms. I would say that in certain areas she held the power of decision and he just went along.

Interview with Yehoshuah Amir

(Translated Buber's Book Kingship of God
into Hebrew.
Taught at Tel Aviv and Ben Gurion Universities.)

Q. When did you first encounter Buber?

A. I was born in Germany in 1911; my father was a rabbi.
When I finished secondary school, Buber's translation
of the Bible was first appearing in print. It made a
great impression on us, and in the youth movement
we were enthralled by this translation. Before that I
knew about Buber and had read some of his writings.
We all learned from him that Judaism not only means
guarding a heritage of the past, but can also be a chal-
lenge for the future. I first saw Buber in the mid 1930s
in Berlin in the Bible evenings that he held.

Q. Did you get to know him?

A. No, I was too bashful and did not belong to the group
led by Menachem Gerson who met with Buber as his
students. I met Buber much later, in Israel, when I
translated some of his writings from German into Hebrew. But to get back to the Bible evenings in Berlin,
they were a great experience for all involved; I sometimes wonder if Buber knew how greatly he influenced us.

Q. I understand that you found it difficult to approach
Buber personally. Was this only a result of your being
bashful?

A. I believe that Buber had a very complex relationship
to his listeners. He seemed to don the cloak of a priest
and to speak like a prophet. His phrases were great to
listen to, but they lacked the simple vitality that one
finds in the writings of Rosenzweig, for instance. Put
differently, I would say that Buber was a great teacher,

but he had no students. There was a feeling that he was great, but that one could not follow him all the way. This attitude is also, I believe, expressed in his writings.

Q. Did you ever meet alone with Buber?

A. Only when I worked on translating his writings. The meetings were cordial; we would sit for an hour and a half and discuss problems of the translation. I remember once asking him, concerning a word in German, whether we should not try and formulate a new Hebrew word for it. I think it was concerning his book *Kingship of God.* He answered, "If there would be many readers for this book, it might be appropriate to formulate a new word, but there will be few readers."

Q. Did you meet with Buber personally in other circumstances?

A. Yes, in two study groups that were held during the Second World War. The first was held in Joseph Bentwich's home, and we discussed religious topics. Most of the participants were people who were linked to the Hebrew University. Buber would come from time to time, and when he spoke, he would get up and explain his view with emotional gestures and prophetic formulations. I particularly remember him lecturing to us that way when we discussed the book of Job. The only person there who could respond to him, and could, at times, show the weakness of Buber's argument, was Julias Gutmann. He was then an old man, a bit bent over, and he often stuttered. But when he answered Buber he hit the mark perfectly.

Q. And what was the second group?

A. When the German army invaded North Africa and we thought that they were on their way to capture Egypt, a rabbi here organized a congregation called *Emet Vee-*

munah (Truth and Belief). He wanted this congregation to prepare its members spiritually for the possibility of a German invasion of Israel. Among the activities of the congregation was a Sabbath afternoon meeting with Buber that was held after the afternoon prayer. The intention of the meeting was that people could speak freely with Buber, and he would prepare them spiritually for any grave developments. I don't remember much of what happened at those meetings, but I do remember that Buber never joined in the afternoon prayer—he would come after it was over. Once, the prayer extended longer than expected and Buber stood outside the synagogue waiting for it to finish. He did not enter. And when the prayer was over, he complained to the rabbi that the congregation had not been punctual in completing its prayers.

Q. Over the years, did you see any changes in Buber?

A. I believe that his manner of presenting himself as a celebrity became more natural to him over the years; hence it did not make people who met him in his later years feel that uncomfortable.

Q. Are you saying that his manner of presenting himself bothered you?

A. Perhaps, but we were also hypnotized by it.

Interview with Joseph Bentwich

*(Principal of a high school in Israel and an editor of
a journal on contemporary Judaism)*

Q. When did you first meet Buber?

A. During the Second World War, from 1941 to 1945,
we organized a group for the study of religion that
met once a month at my home in Jerusalem. We discussed religious texts, and quite frequently Buber
would come to our meetings. Later, when we were
writing the constitution of our group, since we wanted
it to be a formal group, we indicated that members of
the group would be people who lived their faith
through Mitzvoth, through acts and deeds. Ernst Simon indicated that Buber might refuse to join, since
he did not keep Mitzvoth. I replied that Buber could
come and participate without being a formal member
of our group, and that is what happened.

Q. How did Buber contribute to your discussions?

A. I would say that he contributed very little. He always
spoke in what seemed to be mystical language, which
was very unclear to his listeners. At times it seemed
to me that Buber would be using his high-flown language to blow up a balloon, and then Julias Gutmann
would respond with a short reply, that, like a pin,
would let all the air out of what Buber had said. Once
he got Professor Roth angry at him and he told him,
"Buber, you are trying to make yourself into a Mai-
monides, why can't you speak simply like Gutmann?"
Remember, Professor Roth was a professor of
philosophy.

Q. Were these your only encounters with Buber?

A. No, come to think of it, I met Buber before he started
frequenting the meetings of our society. There was a

meeting in Professor Roth's house shortly after Buber came to Israel in the late 1930s. Buber gave a lecture explaining that the Zionist movement had failed to guard spiritually the ethical approach of Judaism, especially in its relations with the Arabs. It was rather farfetched, especially since we all knew that Buber had little experience building relations with Arabs—who knows if he ever met with them to discuss building mutual relations? Moshe Sharet responded—and Sharet grew up among Arabs and spoke Arabic fluently. He told Buber a bit about how difficult it can be to establish any relationship with the Arabs, and said that even if the Arabs did not agree, and did not want us or a relationship with us, we had to continue with the establishing of a Jewish state. I found Sharet very convincing, but I don't think that Buber did.

Q. Did you have any personal encounters with Buber?

A. I believe that I had only two such encounters. Once when I was writing a piece for the Hebrew encyclopedia on education, the editor wanted to cut parts of my article. I appealed his decision and it was turned over to Buber to decide. Buber listened politely and cordially, but did not accept the appeal. When the article appeared, they even cut my name off and indicated that the article had been written by the editorial board. The second meeting had to do with my wanting to publish an anthology of writings from different religions with some explanations. I asked Buber to help me in this endeavor and he politely refused, saying that such a book would take up too much of his time. Perhaps he also didn't like my practical approach to religion.

Q. From all this I understand that you did not appreciate Buber very much?

A. I appreciated his writings and his thoughts, although I didn't like his style. His conception of dialogue is very important, his thoughts on Hasidism, Zionism, philosophy, also. I taught his writings to my pupils in high school, even before they were translated into Hebrew. But his style was overdone. It seemed to indicate that Buber was much too pleased with himself.

Q. Was his style also evident in the way he presented himself?

A. Yes, he was an artist, and that was what turned off many people who wanted simplicity from him. I believe that his style and his manner of presenting himself bombastically has to do with his being in many respects only a half-Jew. After all, he married a Catholic and his entire way of life was not Jewish. All of this kept me at a distance from Buber, even though there were years when we met quite frequently.

Interview with Shalom Ben Chorin

(Writer who wrote a book on Buber)

Q. When did you first hear about Martin Buber?

A. I was born in Munich in 1913, and during my youth I was in a Zionist youth movement called *Kadima*. In the movement we read Buber's books, since he was a central figure in the renewal of Judaism and in the Zionist movement. I first saw Buber when he came to lecture at a youth conference. I was so impressed that I wrote him a letter asking him to meet with me at his convenience. We set up a meeting at a certain hotel at a specific time, but Buber did not show up. I suspect there was a problem, but I never inquired.

Q. When did you become closer with Buber? I understand that you wrote a book about your meetings with him?

A. After Buber reached Israel. I attended all the lectures that he gave on the Bible, and his lectures and meetings at *Emet Veemunah* synagogue, where we also discussed what was going on in the world and in Israel. He also held a Bible study group in his home for a while.

Q. Tell me about your first personal meeting with Buber.

A. I've already written about it in my book: *Zweisprache mit Martin Buber*. It occurred in 1936 when Buber came to visit Jerusalem. I had written to Buber in Heppenheim before he came and asked him some questions in philosophy and theology. Buber wrote back that he could not answer at that moment, and that he would meet with me personally when he reached Jerusalem, and we set up a meeting in his hotel in Jerusalem. At that meeting Buber spoke at length, and with many details, about the problems he was having with his inherited estate in Poland—he had to pay taxes even though he received no income, etc. I was, at first, surprised that Buber spoke about these topics at such length and in such detail. Only later did I understand that Buber was trying to lead me away from abstractions and back to reality. You see, I hadn't written to Buber about my many difficulties in coming to Israel, my not finding a job, and other problems. I had written to him only about abstract topics. By talking about his problems Buber wanted to open my heart, and to give me the opportunity to speak about my own problems. After a few months I told him that I understood his intention in speaking to me this way at our first meeting. He laughed and said, "Maybe it was my intention and maybe it wasn't."

Q. What was the atmosphere in Buber's home?

A. I was impressed by the enormous library that extended over several rooms. Buber always sat behind his large desk. And there was the atmosphere of visiting a very German professor. I believe that Paula contributed to this atmosphere. There were cats in the room and Buber would speak to them. In the summer the window was open and the cats would jump in and out. Once a cat jumped in and Buber asked it, "Where did you come from, I haven't seen you for quite a while." I felt as if the cats understood what Buber said to them. He lived in a house with his granddaughter and great-grandchildren. He used to say, "We don't understand our children, with the grandchildren it is a bit better, and with the great-grandchildren even better." He had a sense of humor. I once asked him a question in theology. He answered, but saw that I did not understand. He then said, "All right, now I'll answer you in non-Buberian language."

Q. So he had patience with your not understanding him?

A. When someone didn't understand him, Buber had great patience. He didn't like intellectuals who paraded with high-flown language, for them he had no patience at all. But when a worker or a housewife didn't understand him, Buber answered with great patience.

Q. Did Buber ever speak to you about his childhood?

A. In my personal meetings with him it did not come up. But at one of his birthday celebrations he told a bit. He said that he had helped his grandfather with Rashi, since Solomon Buber had never learned French, and Rashi often wrote in ancient French, which Martin Buber learned as a child. He also told a story about one of his private tutors. The tutor talked too much and nagged Buber. One day they went for a walk near a lake and Buber pushed the tutor into the water with all his clothes on. After this incident Buber never saw the tutor again.

Q. Did Buber hold birthday parties?

A. They were really get-togethers when he reached a round number of years—65, 70, 75. We would sit together at his house and drink wine.

Q. Do you remember Buber ever getting angry?

A. Only about political matters. Then he would raise his voice and express anger.

Q. Could you visit his house without a specific goal in mind?

A. I respected Buber greatly, and therefore I would never visit him without setting up a meeting. When I called to set up a meeting I always indicated the topic that

I wished to discuss with him. Perhaps I was influenced by the fact that I never heard Buber say *du* to anybody outside his immediate family. He always said *Sie*. Even though he was the philosopher of the I-Thou and had written *Ich und Du*. Ernst Simon knew Buber for fifty years and was close to Buber, but Buber never said *du* to him. The same is true of Hugo Bergmann and Gershom Scholem, whom Buber knew since their youth. Buber always made sure that language would create a distance between himself and others. Perhaps there were instances in which Buber said *du* to a person who was not a member of his family, but I never encountered such an instance. Perhaps he thought that *du* is such a holy word that one can use it only in exceptional cases.

Interview with Ben Ami

*(Painter in St. Gallen, Switzerland,
who met briefly with Buber)*

Q. When did you meet Buber?

A. I met with Buber only twice, on two consecutive days,
when he came to visit Switzerland and to give a lecture at our university some years after the Second
World War. The lecture was fascinating, Buber
seemed to electrify the atmosphere in the large audi-
torium. He read from his writings about Hasidism
and spoke about Hasidism. After the lecture my wife
and I came up to him and I told him that my grandmother was the granddaughter of Rabbi Simha
Bunam, whom Buber admired and wrote about in his
book *Gog und Magog*. Buber smiled warmly. I sensed
that he was very happy that I had come up to him. I
also told him that my name, Ben Ami, is a Hebrew
version of Bunam; he liked that. I had a copy of *Gog
und Magog* in my hand and I asked Buber to autograph
it. He replied that he usually refused to autograph his
books, but in this case he was happy to do so. Paula
looked on as I explained to Buber my family tree start-
ing from Simha Bunam. She seemed to have a penetrating glance. In parting, Buber gave me a reprint of
one of his articles and asked if we could join him and
his wife for breakfast the following morning. What
caught my eye was that Buber was short and not impressive physically, even though one seemed to sense
a divine spark in his eyes.

Q. What happened the next morning?

A. We had breakfast with them at their hotel. We spoke
about general topics and then we accompanied them
to the train station. I perceived a little of the relations

between Buber and Paula. She related to him a bit as if he were a holy person whom she must serve and admire. He accepted her serving and admiring him naturally, as if it was due to him.

Q. Did Buber speak about anything personal with you?

A. No, he spoke in general terms about how a person should relate to others. If I remember well, in the context of Bunam he spoke about serving humanity with modesty. There was something noble about his entire appearance.

Q. Who paid for the breakfast?

A. Neither of us. Buber signed and charged it to the university that was hosting him.

Q. Do you have any other lasting impressions of Buber from those short meetings?

A. Yes. Afterward I felt that Buber seemed to create a circle around himself; no one was allowed to penetrate that circle. Inside the circle he was steeped in a deep personal loneliness that he could share with no other person. And whatever you did you could not get closer to Buber than that circle of loneliness; it had become part of his life. The memory of that circle always accompanies my admiration of his personality and his writings.

Interview with Gavrial Stern

(Journalist in Israel who interviewed Buber several times)

Q. When did you first get to know Buber?

A. I was born in Germany, and I first encountered some of Buber's writings in my grandmother's house. I grew up in an assimilated house, my parents were almost anti-Zionist. When I grew up my views were close to those of the *Werkleute*. I became an active Zionist when Hitler came to power. I was then nineteen years old, and I left Germany for Hachshara in Holland, after which I came to Israel. Although I read books by Buber when I was in Holland, I first saw him at a lecture that he gave in Jerusalem, after he had come to Israel. The lecture was in German. Afterward I heard him in his inaugural lecture at the Hebrew University on Mount Scopus. Later, I began meeting Buber on matters of mutual concern.

Q. During these meetings did you also discuss personal topics?

A. No, I never spoke to Buber about my private affairs. I also did not visit him often; I was hesitant, and didn't want to bother him. But I got to know him through our joint work at the Jewish-Arab Friendship League. I said that I was hesitant to visit him, but I should add that when I did come to him the hesitance disappeared. For instance, I interviewed him three or four times for the newspaper *Baayot*. I remember that when I did some sloppy work Buber was very unhappy about it. Later, when he grew older and would meet me in Jerusalem, he would invite me to his home, and my lasting impression of these meetings is that Buber was a person who knew how to listen. He was also a person who was always trying to get to the truth of a matter, and was even willing to nag you in order to get to that truth. He was also a practical man, especially when dealing with money.

Q. Could you give an example of his being practical?

A. I remember that when the monthly *New Outlook* was established, they asked Buber to come to the first meeting and to give his blessing to the venture. Buber came and spoke about practical things, like the budget, the price of paper, the honorarium for authors, etc. I believe that he did it purposely, since he wanted to examine whether the venture was serious. I also heard that he knew how to give his publishers a difficult time in money matters. I felt that people were jealous of him because he was wealthy and lived in a beautiful house.

Q. Did Buber develop relations with Arabs?

A. People criticized him for not developing relations with Arabs. I think the complaints were unfair. Buber came to Israel at the age of sixty, and he had problems adjusting himself to Israel. I believe that it was very difficult for him to think of developing relations with Arabs during this period of adjustment. He did discuss the need for such relations when he was in Germany, and he personally supported attempts to develop Jewish-Arab relations. In general, Buber was willing to support important causes. When I worked on a team that tried to spread literacy in Israel, Buber came to our opening meeting and spoke warmly in support of such an endeavor.

Q. For some years Buber lived in an Arab section of Jerusalem. What about his relations with Arabs there?

A. That's an interesting story. You see, I helped Buber get a house in Arabic Jerusalem when he had to leave his apartment in Talbiya. He asked me to put an ad in an Arabic newspaper, which I did, not mentioning that the house was for Buber. The ad was answered by a respectable family in Arab Jerusalem—Dr. Djani—whose family were in charge of King David's grave on Mount Zion. Buber lived in that house in Abu Tur from 1944 until 1948, and he had very good relations with the Djani family. In Abu Tur there were few Jews, and when Jewish-Arab relations became hostile in 1948, I once called Buber and asked him whether, for security reasons, he should not think of abandoning his house. He answered, "In Abu Tur there are two parties. One party wants to kill me. The other thinks that it isn't worthwhile to kill me. I believe that the second party is currently prevailing." And he explained why, which I don't remember. But I do remember that he spoke calmly. I also remember that when he finally left Abu Tur, the Djani family and a teacher who lived there took care of Buber's books.

Q. Do you remember Buber ever getting angry?

A. I don't remember him getting angry. He could be demanding, like when he thought I wasn't doing enough to finish something on time.

Interview with Avraham Tsivion

(An Educator who lived in Jerusalem, and consulted with Buber)

Q. How did you get to know Buber?

A. I was attracted to him for a number of reasons. In the 1940s and 50s, education in Israel was collectivistic, which I didn't like, and I found that Buber stressed the individual person. I also liked the fact that Buber was able to give new life to old words whose meaning and sound had been lost. And I was impressed by the fact that Buber had the courage to stand up for things he believed in, like dialogue with Arabs. I knew that because of these views he was not admired in the Israeli streets, and they also did not like his bend toward mysticism.

Q. When did you first meet Buber?

A. I was a student in Haifa and Ernst Simon, who taught there, got us together. I was invited to Buber's house. When I came in and saw his tremendous library I felt that I was entering the realm of spirit. I saw a tremendous head attached to a rather short body, and this added to my feeling that I was sitting in the presence of a Biblical prophet.

Q. Did Buber relate to you personally?

A. Yes, he related to me personally, but I don't remember the details of the first meeting. I perceived that he could listen, but in the second meeting I had with him, I sensed that he often could go into long monologues.

Q. What happened at that second meeting?

A. I came to Buber before leaving for England on a mission sponsored by the Mapai party, in which I was supposed to educate young Zionists in the Diaspora.

I told Buber that I didn't exactly know what to do on this mission, and asked him how I could present the Zionist approach to a group of people who had no interest in it. I said that since I didn't want to fail, perhaps he could give me a formula how not to fail. Here the monologue began. A smile spread on Buber's face and he spoke almost in a whisper: "You're a young man and you want a formula? Let me tell you something. When I was young I liked to be in touch with great people, and to know their views on two matters: truth and religion. But that was worthless and faded like smoke. In those days I often used to walk along Unter den Linden, a main street in Berlin, with my friend Albert Einstein." I was shocked and at that moment Buber's face became serious as he tried to recall the situation. He continued: "I asked him, 'Einstein, my friend, what are you looking for in your world?' He answered, 'Here is the face of the cosmos. I want to cover it with transparent paper and draw on that paper the coordinates of the universe. I lack only one thing and that is what I am seeking: the formula.' " Buber sat up in his chair and continued with his eyes wide open: "I answered him, 'You're asking for too much, Einstein,' and in my heart I thought: 'Chutz-pah'." After this story Buber continued a long monologue about Einstein, pointing out how naive Einstein was in political matters; if someone asked him to sign a petition with the word peace on it he signed immediately. He never asked himself whether the petition served God or the devil. He then quoted a verse from the New Testament that says something to the effect that one should be as innocent as a dove and as cunning as a snake, and finally turned to me and said,

"You want a formula? What a person can do in this world is to struggle to move it just one inch in the right direction, and if he succeeds, he's done much. I wish you success." With that I left. But I felt that I had been at a meeting with the world of spirit.

Interview with Gideon Freudenberg

(He worked with Buber at the Seminar for National Teachers)

Q. When did you first come in contact with Buber?

A. I first heard him when he lectured at a seminar organized by the Moshavim movement. He lectured on the Bible. Later I worked with him at the Seminar for National Teachers. He was the director, later he called himself the president. I was the general manager.

Q. Did he teach there?

A. Yes, he came twice a week to deal with problems of the Seminar and to teach.

Q. How was he as a teacher, an educator?

A. Buber was seventy years old or more, and his students were young. He had problems. My wife heard him in 1923, when he was much younger, and then he was fascinating.

Q. How were your relations with Buber?

A. Good. He was willing to discuss various topics. But he seemed lonely. I once remember, after he was sick with a cold, asking him about his health. He looked at me as if no one had ever asked him such a question.

Q. How did you address him?

A. We spoke Hebrew, so there was no problem. I said you.

Q. Did you ever joke with him?

A. No!

Q. Did Buber have any influence on the other teachers at the seminar?

A. No. There was little contact between the teachers. Only once during the four years of the Seminar did Buber invite us all over to his house for a cup of tea.

Q. Were your contacts with Buber limited to the two days that he taught?

A. No, not at all. Almost every evening he would call me to discuss some minor problem or suggestion, or in connection with a letter he had received. When someone had to sign, Buber emphasized that he only trusted me to sign for him, and that he was ready to sign anything I submitted to him without reading it.

Q. Would you say that Buber was open to his students?

A. No. Definitely not.

Q. Were there any general meetings of the staff?

A. No.

Q. Where would you say that Buber's influence emerged at the Seminar?

A. In two things. He agreed to accept people to the Seminar as students only on the basis of an interview, and not on the basis of certification. And he participated in all the interviews. Second, his name helped establish and support the Seminar, especially in helping cope with budgetary problems. I remember that once we were totally out of money and Buber went to the Jewish agency and notified the treasurer that he would not leave his office until he received the money that the Jewish Agency had promised us. He came back with the check.

Q. Do you remember any incidents that Buber related to you from his life?

A. I remember his telling that once on a trip in Germany he suddenly had a deep feeling of inspiration and immediately knew that God existed.

Q. Did Buber ever tell you about his experiences as an educator?

A. Never. But I think that to some extent his personality educated. Some people at the Seminar did become friendly with him.

Interview with Werner Kraft

(A writer in German, living in Israel. He wrote a book about his meetings with Buber.)

Q. I understand that you wrote a book, *Gespräche mit Martin Buber*, about your meetings with Buber. But there you present primarily a diary of your meetings and not your personal attitudes toward him. Could you go into that a bit?

A. Although I was a specialist in German literature in Germany before Hitler, when I came to Israel I had to work as a laborer. The interest in German literature is what linked me to Buber. I at least felt it important to come to listen to Buber's lectures.

Q. When you met with him, how did you feel?

A. Buber gave people the feeling that they were small compared with him. He did not create an atmosphere of dialogue in which people are equal. Moreover, at times he was not straightforward with me. For instance, he did not like the fact that I continued to be interested in and to dedicate myself to German literature, but he didn't tell me his feeling straightforwardly, but instead needled me about my work.

Q. So you didn't feel close to Buber?

A. I did continue to visit Buber, but I don't think that he was close enough to me to give anything of himself. He was always sort of paternalistic: I'll show you the way of Judaism—but that is not a giving of oneself. I noticed another thing in our conversations, that when Buber began to speak mystically, it was in order to evade relating to God.

Q. Would you say that these responses were typical, or were you a special case?

A. I think Buber tried to let everyone feel his superiority.

I believe perhaps that is the reason he had many relations based on correspondence. Since people are so lonely today, correspondence gives you a link with other people, especially if your links with the people you encounter do not break through this loneliness.

Some Dates in the Life of Martin Buber

1878   February 8th, born in Vienna.

1880   His mother abandons his father. Martin is sent to live with his grandparents, Adelle and Solomon Buber, in Lemburg.

1892   Carl Buber, Martin's father, remarried. Martin moves into his father's home.

1896   Martin Buber commences his university studies in Vienna.

1898   He becomes an ardent Zionist and joins the Zionist movement.

1899   Meets Paula Winkler, they begin to live together.

1899   Speaks at 3rd Zionist Congress.

1900   Son, Raphael Buber, is born.

1901   Daughter, Eve Buber, is born.

1901   Becomes editor of *Die Welt,* the official Zionist weekly.

1902   Resigns editorship of *Die Welt.*

1904   Starts researching Hasidism.

1906–11   Works as an editor and publishes two books of Hasidic tales. Resides in Berlin.

1916   Buber and his family leave Berlin and settle in Heppenheim.

1923   Publication of *I and Thou,* which is recognized as his major book.

1924–29   Works with Franz Rosenzweig on translation of Hebrew Bible into German. After Rosenzweig's death in 1929 Buber continues alone.

1938   Buber, Paula and their two granddaughters move to the land of Israel, where Buber was appointed professor of sociology at Hebrew University.

1951   Buber retires from his position at Hebrew University.

1953   Receives Peace Prize of German Book Trade.

1959   Paula dies in Venice, and is buried there.

1965   June 13, Martin Buber dies in Jerusalem.

Index